Fredericksburg
History & Biography

Volume 14, 2015

Central Virginia
Battlefields Trust

Central Virginia Battlefields Trust, Inc.
Fredericksburg, Virginia

CENTRAL VIRGINIA BATTLEFIELDS TRUST

Board of Directors
Harriett M. Condon
Bradley M. Gottfried
Lloyd B. Harrison, III
Robert Lee Hodge
Peter R. Kolakowski
Robert K. Krick
Kevin Leahy
James M. Pates
Eric Powell
Michael P. Stevens
Thomas A. Van Winkle
Linda P. Wandres

Executive Director
Ben Brockenbrough

Webmaster
Thomas A. Van Winkle

Executive Director
J. Michael Greenfield

Webmaster
Tom Van Winkle

President
Michael P. Stevens

Vice President
Harriett M. Condon

Secretary
Robert K. Krick

Treasurer
Lloyd B. Harrison, III

Editor
Erik F. Nelson

Table of Contents

V   Introductory Notes

9   "No Men…Could Have Accomplished More or Behaved Better." The Battle of Chancellorsville as Reported by Three Soldiers of the 153rd Pennsylvania

By Jeffrey D. Stocker

33   Minutes of the Common Council of the Town of Fredericksburg, 1866-1867.

Typescript corrected and annotated by Erik F. Nelson

105   Fredericksburg's Second Battlefield: Hidden but Not Forgotten

By Erik F. Nelson

131   Southern Exposure: Medal of Honor Recipient Caught Straggling on the March

By Eric J. Mink

137   Index

Property Acquired by the Central Virginia Battlefields Trust

The CVBT has helped to preserve historic terrain at four major battlefields. Over 1,000 acres of critical ground that would otherwise have been lost to development have been acquired in fee simple (sometimes in partnership with other organizations) or have been placed under an easement. The breakdown, by battlefield, is as follows:

FREDERICKSBURG

Willis Hill
Pelham's Corner
Latimer's Knoll
Braehead
Slaughter Pen Farm

CHANCELLORSVILLE

McLaw's Wedge
Nine Mile Run
Talley Farm
Orange Plank Road
Smith Run
May 1 Field
Flank Attack

WILDERNESS

Grant's Knoll
Wilderness Crossroads

SPOTSYLVANIA COURT HOUSE

Po River/Block House Bridge
Harris Farm

Introductory Notes

In its nineteenth year of acquiring and protecting battlefield land, the Central Virginia Battlefields Trust is pleased to present this fourteenth volume of *Fredericksburg History and Biography*. "Dirt and Grass" remain the Trust's watchwords, but the land has a story to tell and we have adopted a literary goal to offer both previously unpublished primary material as well as scholarly work that relate to the land we seek to preserve. The following authors have contributed to this volume:

Jeffrey D. Stocker is a graduate of Muhlenberg College (Magna Cum Laude), where he earned a Bachelor of Arts degree in History. He followed that with a law degree from the Temple University School of Law and is a practicing attorney in Allentown, Pennsylvania. An avid historian and preservationist, Mr. Stocker has been a long-time member of the CVBT. He is the editor of *From Huntsville to Appomattox*, published by the University of Tennessee Press (1996) as part of their "Voices of the Civil War" series. He is also a co-author of *"Isn't This Glorious!"* which was the 2006 winner of the Bachelder-Coddington Literary Award. His latest book, *"We Fought Desperate,"* is a history of the 153rd Pennsylvania Volunteer Infantry Regiment, published in 2014. He is a past president of the Civil War Round Table of Eastern Pennsylvania and resides in Center Valley, PA with his wife. The letters he presents here are from three soldiers who found themselves in the path of Stonewall Jackson's flank attack on May 2, 1863. Many years ago, the CVBT acquired some of the land upon which the experience of the 153rd Pennsylvania unfolded and it is our great pleasure to share these related primary documents. That early CVBT purchase was located north of the Orange Turnpike and has since been transferred to the National Park Service, for inclusion within the Fredericksburg and Spotsylvania National Military Park. Other land acquired south of the Turnpike is still in CVBT ownership and will be transferred when the Park adjusts its authorized boundary and is able to accept it.

Erik F. Nelson is the Senior Planner for the City of Fredericksburg. He is a graduate of the University of California, Santa Barbara, where he earned a Bachelor of Arts as well as a Master of Arts in History. In addition to his extensive planning duties, he is the City Archivist and custodian of the old hand written minute books of Fredericksburg's town council. He has also preserved the handwritten rough drafts of those minutes, which sometimes provide additional information that was inadvertently left out of the minutes copied smooth. This journal has been presenting a full transcription of the old Council minutes, carrying readers through the Civil War in two year increments. This volume covers the years 1866-1867, which reveal how post-war reconstruction began to play out for the local governing body. The editor has also taken it upon himself to look at how the second battle of Fredericksburg has been left out of discussions related to preservation and interpretation. Fredericksburg is known for its concentration of battlefields, where 100,000 soldiers became casualties during the period 1862-1864. Visitors to the Fredericksburg and Spotsylvania National Military Park are invited to see the battlegrounds of Fredericksburg, Chancellorsville, the Wilderness, and Spotsylvania Court House. There is also a fifth battlefield, represented by Salem Church, but that terrain has been lost to houses, commercial strips, and more churches. Fredericksburg's second battle extended across much of the ground related to the first battle of Fredericksburg, but much of those battlegrounds are outside the National Park. Even interpreting the first battle of Fredericksburg proved tricky until significant additions were made to the Park beginning in the 1990s.

Eric J. Mink is a graduate of Mary Washington College, where he earned a Bachelor of Arts in Historic Preservation and American Studies. He grew up in Gettysburg, Pennsylvania and gravitated toward the National Park Service for a professional career. He serves as the cultural resource manager at the Fredericksburg and Spotsylvania National Military Park and is a regular contributor to this journal. The photo he presents here is a well known image of Lieutenant General Ulysses S. Grant and his staff at Massaponax Church, in Spotsylvania County. In the past few weeks, the Army of the Potomac had confronted the Army of Northern Virginia in the Wilderness and at Spotsylvania Court House, sustaining as well as inflicting horrendous casualties. The Union army was pushing south yet again and the series of photos taken at the church capture a few moments of that march. Of interest is a soldier standing in the background who has not only been identified, but whose story is a fascinating microcosm of the nineteenth century American experience. Eric initially posted this story on a blog maintained by the Fredericksburg and Spotsylvania National Military Park and it is an exceptionally neat bit of research that he has generously allowed us to publish.

Erik F. Nelson
Editor

Top: For years, visitors to the Chancellorsville battlefield encountered this castle, incongruously located in the area where Stonewall Jackson launched his flank attack on May 2, 1863. The owners sold military surplus items there as well as historical memorabilia. **Middle**: The CVBT acquired the castle property in 2012 and removed it from the battlefield shortly thereafter. **Bottom**: The restored property is a component of a collection of more than 90 acres the CVBT has assembled in that area, in partnership with the Civil War Trust.

Colonel Charles Glanz, commander of the 153rd Pennsylvania Volunteer Infantry.

"No Men...Could Have Accomplished More or Behaved Better."

The Battle of Chancellorsville as Reported by Three Soldiers of the 153rd Pennsylvania

BY JEFFREY D. STOCKER

When he rode into the clearing around a heretofore-insignificant crossroads mansion called Chancellorsville, early on the evening of April 30, 1863, Major General Joseph Hooker, commander of the Army of the Potomac, must have felt a great deal of satisfaction and pride in both his army and himself. And why would he not have? After all, his plan to move a strong column of infantry on a wide flank march into the rear of the Army of Northern Virginia had so far worked beautifully. Over the past four days, the Union V, XI, and XII Corps had crossed both the Rappahannock and Rapidan Rivers virtually unopposed and now were massed in the vicinity of Chancellorsville. Hooker and his command had stolen a march on the celebrated Robert E. Lee and were now perfectly positioned to cut the Confederate army's vital lines of supply and communication, which stretched by railroad from Fredericksburg to Richmond. With these crucial arteries threatened, Hooker believed that his celebrated opponent "must either ingloriously fly, or come out from behind his defenses and give us battle on our own ground, where certain destruction awaits him."[1]

Unfortunately for the cause of the Union, within the span of less than a week, General Lee and his magnificent Army of Northern Virginia would turn the tables on "Fighting Joe" Hooker and his army. Lee and his chief lieutenant, General Thomas J. "Stonewall" Jackson, planned and executed a

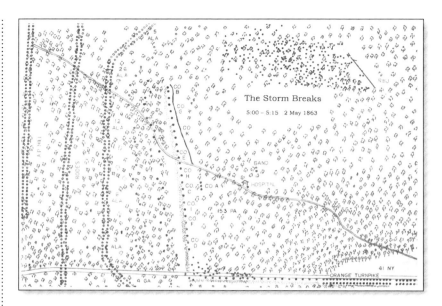

Map showing the position of the 153rd Pennsylvania Regiment as Stonewall Jackson's forces bear down upon them and the extreme right flank of the Union army on May 2, 1863.

brilliant scheme, in which Jackson's Second Corps moved to a point opposite the Army of the Potomac's exposed right flank and then launched a violent, overwhelming assault that turned the tide of the campaign. The blow initially fell on the troops of the First Brigade, First Division of the XI Corps. One of the regiments in this brigade was the 153rd Pennsylvania.

In the early fall of 1862, the 153rd Pennsylvania Volunteer Infantry Regiment had been recruited primarily from Northampton County in southeastern Pennsylvania, to serve for a period of nine months. After being mustered into Federal service, in November 1862, the unit was assigned to the First Brigade of the XI Corps' First Division. As the XI Corps did not participate in the Battle of Fredericksburg, the soldiers of the 153rd had not yet experienced the horrors of Civil War combat. When they bivouacked west of Chancellorsville late on the evening of May 1, 1863, that circumstance would soon change.

On the morning of May 2, the three divisions and four artillery batteries of the XI Corps, numbering approximately 12,000 officers and men, stretched west from the Orange Plank Road down the Orange Turnpike. Most of the corps' units and guns had deployed fronting south. Within the

XI Corps, the responsibility for holding the Army of the Potomac's extreme right flank went to the First Division. Only two regiments from the division's First Brigade, the 153rd Pennsylvania and the 54th New York, faced west, both posted north of the turnpike. Two pieces of the 13th New York Independent Battery, Light Artillery dropped trail in the turnpike itself, also pointing west. The battery's remaining four guns were positioned on the division's left, along the turnpike, facing south. Also stationed on the north side of the turnpike and fronting to the west was Company E of the 45th New York, deployed to the 153rd's left.[2]

Commanding the 153rd on this fateful day was Colonel Charles Glanz, a 39-year-old immigrant from Baden, Germany, who in 1851 had settled in Easton, the seat of Northampton County, where he had opened a brewery.[3] He disposed his unit's ten companies as follows: Positioned to the right (north) of the 45th's Company E, Glanz deployed Company D, followed from left to right by Companies F, I, C, H, E, K, G and B. Company A took a reserve position just behind the regimental line, as a protection for a road that the Pennsylvanians had cut earlier on the morning of May 2, to be used in case of a retreat. The 54th New York was posted to the right and rear of the 153rd.[4]

Late that afternoon, Stonewall Jackson launched his famous flank attack on the XI Corps. As noted above, among the first recipients of the assault were the approximately 700 officers and men of the 153rd Pennsylvania.[5] In the weeks following the battle, many Pennsylvanians put writing instruments to paper to tell their loved ones back in Northampton County what happened on that fateful day. Printed below are letters from three of these men. The first two appeared in *The Easton Express*, while the third was printed in the *Northampton County Correspondent & Democrat*, a German-language newspaper. The author of the first letter, who signed his name "R.", was either Captain John Ricker of Company E, a 38-year-old master carpenter from Easton, or 18-year-old Captain Howard Reeder of Company G, an Easton college student. Company G's Private Stryker Wallace, aged 19, a school teacher from Upper Mount Bethel Township, authored the second letter. Company E's 2nd Lieutenant Paul Bachschmid penned the German-language letter. Born in Leutkirch, Wurttemberg, on February 3, 1818, Bachschmid had immigrated to the United States in 1851, eventually settling in Nazareth, Northampton County, where he had worked as a saloon keeper prior to his enlistment.[6]

Captain John Ricker, Company E of the 153rd Pennsylvania Regiment. Photo courtesy of the Northampton County Historical and Genealogical Society.

Letter from the 153d Regt. Brooke's Station, May 20, 1863

Editor Express:

I am grieved and surprised to hear that there are men at home who are willing to injure the reputation of our regiment by the circulation of slanderous reports which are utterly without foundation. No men situated as the 153d, could have accomplished more or behaved better.[7]

Before the enemy opened upon our front, he had cast eighteen regiments extending for a mile and half, upon our flank and partly in our rear, and then threw his massed troops and heavy columns upon the front of our brigade.[8] The fire from the attack in front was very severe, and at the same time we were enfiladed by a fire passing through our lines from right to left. It was impossible for our brigade successfully to resist this furious and well planned attack from the whole of Jackson's corps. We were in a single line of battle, the men scattered two or three paces apart, so that it was impossible for them to support each other more than skirmishers could. We had two guns of three inch calibre, and ten cavalry under the command of a Sergeant. The other regiments in the brigade (old troops) saw that resistance was hopeless, fell back taking the artillery with them.[9] Had the 153d left with them, a plain statement of the facts would justify them for considering our situation, out-flanked as we were, overwhelmed by ten-fold our number, massed for a crushing attack, almost surrounded, and an enfilading firing without artillery, it is absurd to look for anything but defeat and capture. – Had we stood till every man died in his tracks we could have accomplished nothing. *But the 153d did stand alone.* I saw men among them smiling and joking in that hail of bullets, ball and shell, with all the cool unconcern of veterans. Not a man fired until the order was given. My company's fire was resumed till the enemy was within fifty yards of our line, and it was then delivered with cool and careful aim, told well in the ranks of the enemy. After the second fire, it became a hand–to–hand fight, with pistols and clubbed muskets, and our men gave them as good as they got. Had we met only a thin scattered line of battle, we might at this game bravely held our ground, but before long the weight and pressure of the masses of the enemy forced us back, and the order was given to retreat. Our men even fought as they fell back, and some were then taken prisoners. One of our Captains [was] captured by the collar, and his surrender demanded, but he fought himself loose and escaped.[10]

Captain Howard Reeder, Company G of the 153rd Pennsylvania Regiment. Photo courtesy of the Northampton County Historical and Genealogical Society.

We fought in the woods and the thick heavy undergrowth in our rear was fairly mowed down by the flanking fire of which I have spoken. On Sunday, we were shelled without any harm done, and Sunday, Monday and Tuesday we had skirmishing with the enemy sharpshooters, in which one of our men brought down a "reb" from a treetop. He struck the ground head first.[11] During three days no man could mistake the anxiety of the men for an attack in force. Only when the order was given to recross did I perceive any symptoms of desponding. They longed for the chance to avenge their comrades and regain their ground.

You at home do not know how much sensitiveness the soldier in the field looks to the expressions of opinion from the friends and fellow citizens whom they have left behind; and when men are nobly and bravely doing their whole duty, they feel kingly the deep cruelty of being denounced unjustly by even a small portion of those for whom they are exposing themselves in the field.

—R.

Letter from the 153d Regt.
Camp Potomac Creek, VA, May 8, 1863

We have just returned from a grand parade. It was the grandest that I ever witnessed. Our corps, together with the Fifth and Twelfth, received marching orders on the 26th of last month. We took up the line of march the 27th, towards the Rappahannock by a round about way, crossing the river at Kelly's Ford, and approaching Fredericksburg in the rear of the rebel army. The first we saw of any "rebs" was at the ford, we made them skedaddle double–quick. We crossed the ford on the night of the 28th or the morning of the 29th. We were ordered to fall in at 5 o'clock in the evening (28th) to cross the river, but in consequence of other troops crossing we did not get across till about one or two o'clock at night. It was very dark and we in an enemy's county. – After we were across we waded around through the mud till about 3 o'clock in the morning, and laid down in a meadow until daylight. We were in the advance, but here the 12th corps passed us. We arrived at our place of destination without any fight and took the position assigned to us on the right wing of the corps, the corps being on the right of the Grand Army of the Potomac. Everything passed off quiet until the second of this month, when the enemy attacked us in force on the extreme right. Our boys were deployed as skirmishers; they were driven in, a rebel battery was fired, and some of our fellows on the left of the regiment seeing some rebel pickets, fired, and soon the whole regiment fired.[12] I guess it scared the rebel some, as they fell back. – Capt. Rice, (acting Major), was again sent out with ten men from each company as skirmishers.[13] Our Captain [Howard Reeder] asked the men who wanted to go as skirmishers, and John Ribley was the first to volunteer. The skirmishers were deployed. Soon we heard them fire, and in they came; but poor John Ribley with an arm "dangling" at his side, a ball had struck and broken it. It was the right arm and was afterwards amputated above the elbow.[14] Jacob Rimel fell on the skirmish, supposed to be killed.[15] Peter Kunsman also fell, not heard from.[16] I will send you a list of the killed, wounded and missing. Suffice it to say we lost more than any company in the Regiment, the number being 14.[17] The reason we lost more—ours was the last to run. Our whole regiment acted bravely, and proved what stuff they were made of. The commander of the brigade gives us the praise of doing the best and acting the bravest. One of the New York German Regiments fled without firing a shot. One only fired one round, ours fired five rounds before we left our first position, and then we were ordered to retreat. The "rebs" were in too great force for us, we had to retire, fighting as we fell back. As they came out of the woods our artillery mowed them down like harvest, but they closed up and came rushing on as if life was nothing. Other brigades and divisions joined us, and soon the roar of artillery and the crack of musketry was heard along the whole line. This checked their advance, and darkness terminated the fight. After dark our artillery got into position and commenced playing on them, cutting them at a fearful rate. One of the "rebs" taken prisoner said our artillery killed about three thousand in ten minutes.[18] There was heavy cannonading at about midnight, the rebels getting the worst of it. I slept in the woods close by, and was roused in the morning at daylight of the boom of cannon. The ball was opened for a second day, (being the 3rd of May). I was never awakened by such a revilee before. Deep throated cannon commenced to warble their terrific and mournful sounds, minnie balls, pieces of shells, and messengers of death of all descriptions flew thick and fast. The fight grew hotter and hotter, until finally it raged for miles along the whole line. It became horrible beyond description. The enemy acted very brave. We having the most artillery mowed them down by battalions, but yet the vacancy was filled by human beings not fearing death, and having in their hearts the hellish design of overthrowing the government of their fathers. I talked with men who were in the Bull Run fight, and they say that it was not as terrific as this. Our boys worsted the enemy and drove them back.[19] I met some of the boys of our regiment and company and conducted them to the hospital. Saw lots of wounded soldiers there. It would elicit pity, if not draw tears of sympathy, to see such a lot of mangled humanity, wounded in every place and in every form. The hospital was close by the river, (Rappahannock.) We were not there long before the sick and wounded were sent across the river, for fear we would be shelled by the rebels. Our corps hospital was stationed on the opposite side of the river. I slept along the fence close by the hospital, with nothing under me but some pieces of rails, and nothing over me but a piece of a tent, and that not half of the time, because there were three of us under it, and it was not large enough to cover us all properly. David Eilenberger[20] and Wm. Jennings[21] were with me. We were aroused in the morning (the 4th) by the firing and bursting of a shell in our vicinity. We were inclined to lay still, but the bursting of a second, and finally a succession of shells, soon told what was the matter. A rebel battery was shelling our hospital and supply train. You had better believe there was some skedaddling done. The shells passed over our hospital and consequently did not do us any harm, but killed several men beyond us. [T]he battery was soon silent, and soon came the news that our cavalry had slipped in behind the battery, surprised and took it. I saw some of the prisoners, and our boys put it to them about the mean trick of firing on hospitals. They did not say anything, believing, I guess, that it was little business.[22] I was not hurt in the least, although I heard the bullets buzz and shells whistle. Our principal surgeon, Dr. Neff, is missing.[23] Col. Glantz is among the missing, but it is supposed that the Doctor and Colonel were taken prisoners for the Colonel was wounded in the foot and the last that was seen of them they were behind [the] battery. The Colonel could not get along any further, and the Doctor was trying to dress his wound. [The] battery was captured, and the probability is that the Colonel and Doctor were taken prisoners together. I hope it is only so, for they are missing, and would rather they would be prisoners than killed.[24] I do not know what the result of the fighting is, but I do know the rebels were handled rough the second day and driven from their position. We have recrossed the river. I do not know what it is for, but I think for some reason known only to Gen Hooker. We are at the same camp, at Potomac Creek, but I understand we are under marching orders. I suppose you hear a good deal about the 11th corps running, I tell you the boys of this corps done what they could. They were overpowered, and it is the fault of the Generals not knowing what force was coming on us. Our scouts should have felt and ascertained the strength of the enemy.[25]

—W.

May 20, 1863
From the Northampton Regiment Camp near Potomac Creek Bridge

My Dear Mr. Cole [editor]!
Since my last letter much has changed in our regiment. As you know, we were at that time already under marching orders, and had made ourselves ready for starting as soon as needed. On the 18th of April there was a brigade drill, and, at the same time, the pontoon bridges in the vicinity of Fredericksburg were set up for which we had to engage 2 of our companies for protective cover. Penton's shipment made us aware that something was in the works in the near future. On the 22nd the long-awaited paymaster arrived here and opened his beneficent hand in order to let flow the large and small greenbacks among all the soldiers; whoever approached him with an anxious expression, a dry throat, suppressed emotion and expectant hopes-even bloodthirsty soldiers-were affected by the sight of the splendid greenbacks and everyone-for all of 2 months-remained satisfied. On the 25th about 200 men in our regiment had to be on picket duty when we received orders to meet up with the army the next morning in order to cross the Rappahannock. Already early in the morning, before our departure, the Twelfth Corps passed us. Shortly thereafter, we were brought a mile from our picket posts by Stafford, thrust together with our brigade and marched to Roderman's Ford (not far from Kelly's Ford) where we met up in the valley with 3 army corps (through a hilly chain bordered by the Rappahannock). The day had become quite warm and our troops started to throw off nonessentials-many coats and blankets were already visible on the road. At midnight we crossed the Rappahannock silently; the bridges were knocked down during the night. It was dark and hazy. Our march went through swamps and bogs; we often sank to our knees. Then we camped on a hill the rest of the morning until about 10 am. Fortunately, the 3rd Corps had managed the crossing successfully. On the 29th at about 2:30 am, we passed the Rapidan River. The Rebels had destroyed all bridges, plank roads and telegraphs. On the following morning, Jackson wanted to go across the Rapidan; 71 Rebels had already started to build a bridge for him when they were surprised by our troops and were captured.

Already on the 30th, we expected a battle to develop but the enemy never appeared in plain sight. We camped the night about 2 miles from the Fredericksburg railroad, and I learned that our strength came from

3 army corps with about 45,000 men, namely, the 5th 11th and 12th Corps. On Friday, May 1st around noon the cannonade began; about 200 shots were exchanged. Steinwehr's[26] sharpshooters trained their fire on the enemy's artillery..[W]e took 700 prisoners and 2 cannon. On May 2nd we sent out our skirmishers. At 3:30 we initiated the first volley against the enemy, after which our skirmishers returned. Our regiment was in the first line, somewhat in the center; our brigade (with 2 cannon) was supposed to be able to stop an army of perhaps 30,000 men. We shot 4 rounds. The bullets and shells flew in a heavy volley and around us the artillery was silent. [T]he enemy went around us on the right flank. Both this and the left gave way.[27] Our boys fired their weapons and then made their way as quickly as possible out of the smoke and fire. In vain the officers of the brigade tried to organize a stop to runaways and to assemble together those deserting until they had the first battery in the rear.[28] We were ordered, if we could no longer hold out or avoid being pushed back by superior forces, to fall back to the second line, but my God! Far and wide there was no second line to be seen. They had already gotten to the bottom of the valley before our regiment realized that the first line was broken, and had skedaddled before even firing a shot.[29] I saw our Northampton boys stand and fire until they were almost surrounded by the enemy, then they did as the others. They tried to save their life or freedom. The next corps withstood the barrage, and frightful fire from the approaching batteries was directed into the enemy's ranks and thousands lost their lives that night. We finally got our boys organized that same evening and continued our march forward. The army corps received new orders and we encamped that night thick in the woods, in which the 153rd received the first shots. Once more shells and grenades were fired from both sides as if it were the Last Judgement until late into the night. Finally the bloody spectacle was over and an unnatural quiet crept into the morning. The battlefield was in the hands of the Rebels; our dead and wounded had to be left behind but we mourned many sad casualties, especially our dear Colonel Charles Glanz, of whom we knew was wounded in arm and leg but nothing further was known of his whereabouts.[30] I give you below a report of the dead, wounded and missing inasmuch as I was able to learn up to today. The battlefield lay to the left of Chancellorsville. On the 3rd we marched a few miles further, in the vicinity of Hooker's Headquarters. We applied ourselves to building breastworks, and in the morning at 10 o'clock, today's battle opened with a vigorous cannonade.[31] A crowd of prisoners

were taken, among whom were some women. Many wounded were carried past us to the hospital and today the Rebels pulled back. This time we did not immediately come into combat, although the bomb shells flew back and forth over our heads like hail. Our regiment positioned itself as skirmishers in the woods and many bullets flew, fired by inexperienced hands. We were now near the United States Ford which we had to cover.[32] Since Col. Glanz and also Lt. Col. Dachrodt were wounded, we were, since the 3rd of May, commanded by Major Frueauff.[33] We received crackers, later also meat, crackers, sugar and coffee. On the 4th the weather became very unpleasant; it rained for a couple of days and was very cold. The soldiers trembled in their wet clothes, standing the whole night before the breastworks, without fire or blankets. Then, in the night of the 6th, we again advanced. In the morning at about 2 o'clock, we marched off, crossed the Rappahannock around 6 o'clock, going through deep swamps and horrible, barrel-deep mire along the entire route. During our crossing, the Rebels maintained a hearty fire which was an impediment to us even from afar. While on march, troops went in search of some half-burnt tents and rucksacks which the Rebels had cast off behind them–tents, rucksacks, barrels, drums, etc.–and afterwards forgot to retrieve. Such things were seen as being useful. We notified everyone and gave orders that we would be able to return to our old camp, even on this same evening despite the rain. On the 6th, in the evening, we re-entered our self-destroyed camp.[34] One adjusted now as best as possible and looked forward to the future in the hope that the next encounter with the enemy would have a successful outcome. Today we already received orders to be ready to march at a moment's notice.

                              Your most humble
                              Paul Bachschmid, Lieutenant Co. E

With the battle ended and the survivors of the 153rd back in their camp at Brooke's Station, it was time to take stock of the cost. In the *Official Records,* the regiment's casualties are given as 6 killed, 40 wounded and 39 captured or missing, for a total of 85. A careful study, however, reveals that these figures are much too low. At Chancellorsville, the unit actually lost 16 men killed or mortally wounded, 5 officers and 34 men wounded and 3 officers and 54 men captured; of the latter, 17 of the 54 men had sustained wounds before being taken prisoner. Thus, out of approximately 700 officers and men present at the battle, 112, or 16 percent, had been lost.[35]

The men of the 153rd Pennsylvania were now veterans. They had heard the rattle of musketry and the roar of cannons, had witnessed their friends and relatives drop dead beside them or fall wounded, weltering in blood and gore. Despite their courage, they had been routed and scattered in disorder in dense, dark woods. Many had been taken prisoner. Those who remained, the ones who had returned to their camp at Brooke's Station, mourned those who had been lost and contended with the bitter taste of defeat. A little over two months later, on July 25, 1863, with their term of service expired, the soldiers of the 153rd Pennsylvania Volunteer Infantry Regiment returned to a welcome-home ceremony in Easton, greeted and feted by thousands of happy friends and relatives. Before that joyous occasion though, the Pennsylvanians would pass through one more fiery trial, one that took place on the hills and fields outside a small Pennsylvania town called Gettysburg.[36]

❧ NOTES ☙

1. Stephen W. Sears, *Chancellorsville* (Boston/New York: Houghton Mifflin Company, 1996), pp. 141-153, 161-166, 170-171, 191-192; *The War of the Rebellion: A Compilation of Official Records of the Union and Confederate Armies* (Washington, D.C.: U.S. Government Printing Office, 1880-1901), series 1, vol. 25, pt. 1, p. 171 (hereafter cited as *OR*. Unless otherwise noted, all subsequent citations are from series 1).

2. John Bigelow, *The Campaign of Chancellorsville: A Strategic and Tactical Study* (New Haven: Yale University Press, 1910), map facing p. 274; Oliver O. Howard, "The Eleventh Corps at Chancellorsville," in Robert U. Johnson and Clarence C. Buel, eds., *Battles and Leaders of the Civil War.* 4 vols. (New York: Thomas Yoseloff, 1956), pp. 192-193 (hereafter cited as *Battles and Leaders*); *OR*, vol. 25, pt. 1. P. 628; Augustus Horstmann reminiscences, copy courtesy Kathryn Lerch; Andrew Searles article in undated issue of *The Boston Journal*.

3. Charles Glanz pension file, Record Group 15, National Archives and Record Administration (hereinafter cited as RG, NARA); William H. Egle, *The History of Northampton County, Illustrated, 1877* (Philadelphia and Reading: Peter Fritts, 1877), p. 273; *Bethlehem Daily Press,* July 25, 1880.
4. Charles Glanz letter to Governor Andrew Curtin dated June 2, 1863, contained in 153rd Pennsylvania Regimental Files, Pennsylvania State Archives, Harrisburg (hereafter cited as Glanz letter, PSA); statement of George Young contained in Andrew Burt pension file, RG 15, NARA.
5. The figure of approximately 700 officers and men is given in Rev. W. R. Kiefer, assisted by Newton H. Mack, *History Of The One Hundred and Fifty-third Regiment Pennsylvania Volunteer Infantry Which was Recruited in Northampton County, PA 1862-1863* (Easton: The Chemical Publishing Co., 1909), p. 19 (hereafter cited as Kiefer, *History*), and is substantiated by documentation found in the Pennsylvanians' pension files, compiled service records and medical card files, RG 15 and 94, NARA.
6. The exact date of the edition, or editions, of *The Easton Express* in which the first two letters appeared is unknown, since all issues for the 1863 run of the newspaper are no longer extant. Clippings which contained the letters were found in the Weaver Collection, Northampton County Historical and Genealogical Society, Easton (hereafter cited as WC, NCHGS). The third letter was printed in the May 28, 1863 issue of the *Northampton County Correspondent & Democrat.* John Ricker, Howard Reeder and Paul Bachschmid pension files, RG 15, NARA; *Southtown* [Illinois] *Economist,* May 22, 1940; obituary clipping printed in unknown edition of *The Washington Star,* WC, NCHGS.
7. Beginning immediately after the battle, the Northern press began blaming the XI Corps for the army's latest defeat. For example, in an article printed in the May 5, 1863 issue of the *NEW YORK TIMES,* a correspondent called the corps' troops "retreating and cowardly poltroons." This piece was reprinted in the May 14, 1863 issue of *The Easton Argus.* In the weeks following the battle, dozens of articles and editorials containing such denunciations appeared in newspapers all across the loyal states. In addition, in letters to the home front, many of their fellow soldiers in the Army of the Potomac contributed their own statements of condemnation against the troops of the XI Corps. Naturally, as soon as they got wind of the rising tide of castigation being directed at them, many men in the

153rd quickly responded to attempt to refute the charges of cowardice being hurled against their corps. *The Easton Argus,* May 14, 1863.

8. Brigadier General Robert Rodes' division, five brigades of Alabamians, Georgians and North Carolinians, numbering almost 8,000 officers and men, formed the first line of Stonewall Jackson's attack. Facing east, from left to right, Rodes deployed his troops as follows: On the far left was Brigadier General Alfred Iverson's brigade of four North Carolina regiments, followed successively by a brigade of five regiments of Alabamians led by Colonel Edward O'Neal, four Georgia regiments under the command of Brigadier General George Doles and another brigade of four Georgia regiments commanded by Brigadier General Alfred Colquitt; four regiments of North Carolinians commanded by Brigadier General Stephen Ramseur were positioned to Colquitt's brigade's rear. Across his divisional front, General Rodes posted a "line of sharpshooters…almost 400 yards in advance." The 4th Georgia, the left regiment of Doles' brigade, rested its left flank on the Orange Turnpike. In the ensuing assault, O'Neal's Alabama brigade struck the 153rd Pennsylvania and the 54th New York head-on, and lapped far around the New Yorkers' right flank. *OR,* vol. 25, pt. 1, pp. 940, 941, 947, 969.

9. In the first fire from the advancing Confederates, a musket ball struck Lieutenant Colonel Charles Ashby, the 54th's commander, in the face, inflicting a severe wound and knocking him unconscious. Totally surprised by the Rebel onslaught and now leaderless, the entire regiment broke and fled to the rear, leaving the 153rd's right flank completely exposed. Charles Ashby pension file, RG 15, NARA; William Burghart letter to Augustus C. Hamlin dated November 2, 1891, Fredericksburg and Spotsylvania National Military Park (hereafter referred to as FSNMP).

10. Unfortunately, the identity of this captain is unknown.

11. By 3 a.m. on the morning of May 3, the entire XI Corps, or rather what remained of it, had been reformed, moved to the army's left and placed along the Mineral Spring Road, which ran in a northeast direction from the vicinity of Chancellorsville toward the Rappahannock River. The men of the 153rd spent the next three days deployed in the shelter of some entrenchments, engaged in desultory firing with Confederate skirmishers. Bigelow, *The Campaign of Chancellorsville,* p. 343 and map facing p. 346; William Simmers and Paul Bachschmid, *The Volunteer's Manual; or, Ten Months with the 153d Penn'a Volunteers, Being a Concise Narrative of*

the Most Important Events of the History of Said Regiment (Easton: privately printed, 1863), pp. 24-25 (hereafter cited as Simmers and Bachschmid, *The Volunteer's Manual*).

12. Near mid-day on May 2, a party of Confederate cavalry advancing east on the Orange Turnpike encountered skirmishers from the First Brigade of the XI Corps' First Division. A brief volley of shots ensued, which included a short artillery exchange between the two guns of the 13th New York Independent Battery Light Artillery posted in the turnpike and some Confederate pieces. Back on the 153rd's main line, Lieutenant Colonel Jacob Dachrodt, stationed on the regiment's left flank, gave the command to fire. Augustus Horstmann reminiscences, copy courtesy Kathryn Lerch; Stryker Wallace diary, Henry Marx Room, Easton Public Library, Easton.

13. In response to the firing initiated by Lieutenant Colonel Dachrodt, Colonel Leopold von Gilsa, the commander of the First Brigade of the XI Corps' First Division, in a great wrath, ordered the firing to cease. (Von Gilsa, who had posted himself directly behind the 153rd, was angry that the regiment had opened fire without his orders.) To prevent another such occurrence, Colonel von Gilsa sent out a heavier skirmish line, composed of a detail of ten volunteers from each company of the 153rd, plus a company each from the 45th and 54th New York. Captain Owen Rice of Company A, a 26-year-old former teacher from Nazareth, had command of the 153rd's skirmishers. At this time, the 153rd's Major John Frueauff was serving as Acting Assistant Inspector General on the First Division's staff, which meant that Captain Rice, as the regiment's senior captain, was "acting Major." *The Moravian,* June 11, 1863; Theodorus Weaver diary, Randy Hackenberg Collection, U.S. Army Heritage and Education Center, Carlisle; Owen Rice, *Afield with the Eleventh Corps at Chancellorsville* (Cincinnati: H. C. Sherrick and Co., 1885), pp. 376-377 (hereafter cited as Rice, *Afield*); Augustus Horstmann reminiscences, copy courtesy Kathryn Lerch; Searles article, *The Boston Journal*; William Burghart letter to Augustus Hamlin dated November 2, 1891, A.C. Hamlin papers, FSNMP; Owen Rice pension file, RG 15, NARA; Ethan Allen Weaver, *Owen Rice: Christian, Scholar, Patriot* (Germantown: privately printed, 1911), pp. 7-10; Daniel R. Gilbert, sr., ed., *Freddy's War: The Civil War Letters of John Frederick Frueauff* (Bethlehem: Moravian College, 2006), p. 163 (hereafter cited as Gilbert, *Freddy's War*); John Frueauff compiled service record, RG 94, NARA.

"No Men...Could Have Accomplished More or Behaved Better"

Ethan A. Weaver is shown in this 1890 photo standing at the position of the 153rd Pennsylvania Regiment in the flank attack area of the Chancellorsville battlefield. He was the son of Sergeant William H. Weaver, Company A, who was captured on May 2, 1863. The younger Weaver spent his adult life collecting documentation (letters, diaries, photos, etc.) of his father's regiment. This material, which ended up being four bound volumes, is held by the Northampton County Historical and Genealogical Society. Photo courtesy of the Northampton County Historical and Genealogical Society.

14. Private John Rible (or Ripley), a 44-year-old married laborer from Upper Mount Bethel Township, was struck in the right arm and back by shell fragments. His arm was later amputated 4 inches below the shoulder. In 1864, Rible, who never wore a prosthetic device, began collecting a disability pension of $8.00 per month from the Federal government. Convulsions caused his death at his home in Stone Church, Pennsylvania, on April 27, 1891. John Rible pension file, RG 15, NARA.

15. After his death in action at the age of 27, the widow of Private Jacob Reinell (or Reimel) received a Federal survivor's pension of $8.00 per month. Jacob Reinell pension file, RG 15, NARA.
16. Twenty-four year old Peter Kunsman had been killed in action. He had left behind his family in Upper Mount Bethel Township, where he worked as a carpenter, to enlist in Company G. After his death, the unmarried sergeant's mother collected a monthly Federal survivor's benefit of $8.00. Peter Kunsman pension file, RG 15, NARA; Peter Kunsman compiled service record, RG 94, NARA.
17. Actually, at the Battle of Chancellorsville, Company A suffered 23 casualties, of which 3 were fatal, and Company I lost 18, with no fatalities. Private Wallace was correct in his assertion that Company G had 14 casualties, of which 3 were fatal. These figures have been compiled from documentation found in the Pennsylvanians' pension files, RG 15, NARA, as well as their compiled service records and medical card files, RG 94, NARA.
18. As the victorious Confederates debouched from the woods west of the clearing around Chancellorsville, massed Union artillery pieces, mainly from the XII Corps, supported by some rallied remnants of the XI Corps, opened fire and helped to check the Rebel advance. Howard, "The Eleventh Corps at Chancellorsville," *Battles and Leaders,* vol. 3, pp. 198-199.
19. The thundering of the guns that the Pennsylvanians heard early that morning signaled the onset of fierce fighting that took place in and around Chancellorsville. Despite the best efforts of units from the II, III, V and XII Corps, by the time the combat ended later on May 3, a series of violent Confederate attacks had forced the Unionists out of their positions and into a salient north of Chancellorsville. Sears, *Chancellorsville,* pp. 308-366.
20. Sometime during the course of the chaotic retreat following Jackson's assault, a horse fell on Corporal David Eilenberger of Company G, a 30-year-old laborer from Upper Mount Bethel Township, injuring his right hip. After a short stay at the XI Corps hospital for the treatment of his injury, as well as the effects of chronic diarrhea, he returned to duty and completed his term of service. Eilenberger died at his home in Northampton County on June 27, 1905. David Eilenberger pension file, RG 15, NARA; David Eilenberger compiled service record and medical card file, RG 94, NARA.

21. During the fighting on May 2, a shell fragment struck 24-year-old farm laborer Sergeant William Jennings of Company G, a native of Upper Mount Bethel Township, in the back of the left shoulder, the impact of which briefly knocked him unconscious. Helped off the field by a comrade, he received treatment in various military hospitals not only for his wound, but also for rheumatism, chronic diarrhea and debility, for most of the rest of his service. In 1885, Jennings began collecting a Federal disability pension of $2.00 per month, which, by 1913, had been increased to $22.50 per month. He died from the effects of paralysis in Bangor, Northampton County, on November 24, 1925. William Jennings pension file, RG 15, NARA, William Jennings compiled service record and medical card file, RG 94, NARA.

22. The XI Corps hospital, although established on the north side of the Rappahannock River, proved to be too close to the battle area. On May 4, some 13 pieces of Confederate artillery began shelling Union ammunition and supply trains passing near the hospital grounds; several errant rounds exploded too close for comfort to the wounded and those attending them. Sears, *Chancellorsville,* p. 390.

23. The chief surgeon of the 153rd was Dr. Henry Neff, a 41-year-old native of Huntingdon County, Pennsylvania. After being taken prisoner, Dr. Neff was conveyed to Richmond, where he was held in Libby Prison for several weeks before being paroled and returning to Union lines. Suffering from chronic diarrhea and jaundice, Neff was granted a furlough home to recover from his ailments; he never returned to duty with the regiment. In 1867, Dr. Neff began collecting a monthly disability stipend of $18.75 from the Federal government. On February 21, 1868, Henry Neff died at his home from the effects of lung disease. Henry Neff pension file, RG 15, NARA; Henry Neff compiled service record and medical card file, RG 94, NARA.

24. After "waiting in vain for orders to retreat," Colonel Glanz, "under the most murderous fire [and] seeing no advantage in continuing the fight, but only danger to be entirely cut off of the chance to retreat," ordered his men to fall back. On foot, Glanz then tried to make his way to the rear. Despite having his sword scabbard struck by several bullets and being hit by a spent ball under the right arm which bruised but did not cut the skin, the full-bearded former brewer remained unscathed. In a letter to his wife written 11 days after the battle, a Pennsylvanian painted this sad

picture of the colonel: "The last we saw of him he was standing against a tree supposed to be wounded. The tears were rolling down his face when he said, 'My God, what has become of my regiment.'" Regarding the circumstances of his capture, Glanz later reported, "I was surrounded nearly at the edge of the woods [behind the 153rd's position] and near the new road, which had been cut [by his regiment] in the forenoon..." The colonel was conveyed to a farm in the rear, where he and his fellow captives were confronted by several "infuriated rebel ladies," as he later termed them, who "address[ed] us prisoners in most bitter terms, hoping that this would be a good lesson for us and hoping that we do better in future and not come to Virginia again." Suddenly, a stray artillery projectile struck one of the building's chimneys, shattering it. A stone fragment hit Glanz in the right side of the head, inflicting a severe bruise. The dazed officer was then sent further to the rear. By May 7, Charles Glanz had arrived in Richmond, where he became an inmate of Libby Prison. Exchanged on May 23, 1863, suffering hepatitis and kidney disease; the enfeebled Colonel Glanz never resumed command of the regiment. After his discharge in July 1863, he returned to Easton. In 1879, the year after losing his brewery in an economic downturn, Charles Glanz began collecting a Federal monthly disability benefit of $30.00. On July 24, 1880, he died from the effects of kidney and liver disease. Charles Glanz letter to Governor Andrew Curtin dated June 2, 1863 contained in 153rd Pennsylvania Regimental Files, PSA; Charles Glanz letter dated May 27, 1863 printed in *The Easton Argus,* June 4, 1863; Kiefer, *History,* p. 249; Charles Glanz pension file, RG 15, NARA; Charles Glanz compiled service record and medical card file, RG 94, NARA.

25. In fact, throughout the afternoon of May 2, many different officers and men of the XI Corps "felt and ascertained the strength of the enemy," and sent several increasingly urgent warnings of the Confederate presence to headquarters. For example, in a note that he timed at 2:45 p.m., Captain Owen Rice, in command of the 153rd's skirmishers, wrote, "A large body of the enemy is massing in my front. For God's sake, make dispositions to receive him!" Colonel von Gilsa, the recipient of this communication, personally took it to XI Corps headquarters, where he, and it, was summarily dismissed. Rice, *Afield,* p. 379.

26. Brigadier General Adolph von Steinwehr commanded the XI Corps' Second Division during the Chancellorsville campaign. *OR,* vol. 25, pt. 1, p. 645.

27. Quickly taking advantage of the collapse of the 54th New York, the 5th Alabama, the regiment positioned on the left of O'Neal's brigade's advancing line, "wheeled to the right [and opened] a most destructive fire" on the 153rd's right flank. Deployed to the Pennsylvanians' left, the 45th New York was assaulted in its front by the 3rd Alabama, the right unit of O'Neal's brigade. In addition, the New Yorkers also had to contend with Doles' Georgia brigade, which extended well south of the Orange Turnpike. In the face of such overwhelming odds, after a brief resistance, the 45th broke and fled to the rear. The Georgians then seized the two pieces of the 13th New York Independent Battery Light Artillery posted in the turnpike. General Doles quickly ordered the 21st Georgia to wheel to the left and open an enfilading fire on the 153rd's left flank. Alone in the midst of a cul de sac of smoke, fire and death, the Pennsylvanians stood no chance. *OR,* vol. 25, pt. 1, pp. 958, 967, 970.

28. Within 10 minutes, and quite possibly less, from the time that the men of the 153rd first came under fire, their regimental line was completely shattered. No longer were the Pennsylvanians a disciplined body of troops; they were now a disorganized mass of fugitives seeking a place of safety. One man succinctly remembered, "There was a great excitement." Another later added, "[S]ome ran this way and some that…" Simmers and Bachschmid, *The Volunteer's Manual,* p. 23; statement in Aaron Sandt pension file, RG 15, NARA; Kiefer, *History,* p. 150.

29. Lieutenant Bachschmid was too harsh with this statement. In fact, the units of the Second Brigade of the XI Corps' First Division had been hurriedly moved forward as a support, but were quickly swept away in the furious Confederate assault. These troops fought bravely, but were overcome by the same factors that had crushed the division's First Brigade, namely being confronted by vastly superior numbers in a bad position to defend. *OR,* vol. 25, pt. 1, pp. 637-644.

30. See endnote #24.
31. See endnote #19.
32. See endnote #11.

33. Early on the morning of May 3, upon learning that Colonel Glanz was missing and Lieutenant Colonel Dachrodt was wounded and incapacitated, Major Frueauff formally requested permission to be allowed to leave his position on the staff of the First Division and return to duty with the 153rd. Permission being granted, the major assumed command of what remained of the regiment. Gilbert, *Freddy's War*, p. 177.
34. Prior to setting out on the march early on the morning of April 27, the Pennsylvanians had broken up their winter encampment near Brooke Station, believing that they had seen the last of it. Unfortunately, this supposition proved incorrect.
35. *OR,* vol. 25, pt. 1, p. 182. The casualty figures have been determined from a review of the individual soldiers' pension files, compiled service records and medical card files, RG 15 and 94, NARA.
36. In the course of the three days' fighting at Gettysburg, the 153rd lost 53 killed or mortally wounded, 122 wounded and 123 captured (47 of the 123 taken prisoner had been wounded before their capture), for a total of 298 casualties. The casualty figures have been computed from a review of the individual soldiers' pension files, compiled service records and medical card files, RG 15 and 94, NARA.

In the fighting on July 1, a musket ball struck Captain John Ricker in his lower left leg, which fractured the bone and left him unable to walk. Falling into Confederate hands, Ricker was carried to a farmhouse, where he received some rudimentary care. Paroled when the Army of Northern Virginia retreated, Ricker was transported back to Easton, where he received his army discharge. In September 1863, he filed for a Federal disability pension, which, when granted, began paying him a monthly stipend of $10.00. In the post-war years, Ricker tried to help several old comrades who had also applied for pensions by testifying on their behalf. One pension examiner, who was clearly not impressed with the former captain, noted, "He almost appears to be kind of a blockhead-drunk most of the time." John Ricker's life ended on June 14, 1906, at a hospital in Easton, to which he had been admitted after fracturing his ribs and left hip in two separate falls in the weeks preceding his death. Howard Reeder, Stryker Wallace and Paul Bachschmid all remained unscathed in the firestorm of Gettysburg. Following his discharge, Reeder graduated from Harvard University School of Law and subsequently hung out his shingle in Easton. He eventually became a state superior court judge. Judge Reeder died of pneumonia in Easton on December 28, 1898, just 17 days after his 55th birthday. Stryker Wallace worked for the U. S. Treasury Department in the immediate post-war period. After becoming a minister in the Presbyterian Church, he moved to Illinois and became a pastor. On May 14, 1940, Stryker Wallace died at the age of 96 at his home in Cook County; at the time of his death, he was simultaneously working on his memoirs and an American biographical dictionary. In 1882, afflicted with rheumatism, piles and the effects of a hernia that he had initially incurred on a march after Gettysburg, Paul Bachschmid began collecting a Federal disability pension of $11.50 per month, which supplemented his income generated by his Nazareth, Pennsylvania, floral business. On February 29, 1908, Bachschmid died in Washington, D.C. He was laid to rest in Arlington Cemetery, the only former member of the 153rd Pennsylvania to repose there. John Ricker pension file, RG 15, NARA; *The Easton Express,* June 14, 1906; *The Easton Daily Express,* December 29, 1898; *Southtown* [Illinois] *Economist,* May 22, 1940; Paul Bachschmid pension file, RG 15, NARA; obituary clipping printed in unknown edition of *The Washington Star,* WC, NCHGS.

Trees still grace the sidewalk in front of the Fredericksburg Baptist Church (constructed in 1854-55).

Minutes of the Common Council of the Town of Fredericksburg, 1866-1867

TRANSCRIBED AND ANNOTATED BY ERIK F. NELSON

In the immediate aftermath of the Civil War, the town of Fredericksburg stood devastated. It had been a battleground and become a cemetery. As citizens rebuilt homes and businesses, their local government had to figure out how to rebuild the community. Wrecked vessels sunk at the town wharves, for instance, posed an immediate obstacle to the restoration of some level of maritime trade. The Council's convoluted method of paying for that critical work without adequate resources is detailed herein. The town fathers also had to consider how best to drain a marsh running through the town (where Federal assault columns had foundered). They also needed to find and obtain affordable fire-fighting equipment.

At the state and federal levels of government, the post-war emphasis was on rebuilding the wrecked South and making sure the political ends for which the war was fought (and which kept changing) were not subsequently lost. Reconstruction is the term used to define this era and it actually began during the war. President Abraham Lincoln installed military governors in the occupied parts of Tennessee, North Carolina, Louisiana, and Virginia, as a war measure to try to destabilize the Confederacy. The Virginia governor was Francis H. Pierpont, a Lincoln supporter from the area of Virginia that became West Virginia. As the end of the war approached, there were many unresolved issues that needed immediate attention. The Emancipation Proclamation, for instance, had helped to undermine the Confederacy, but the legal status of the freed slaves had yet to be resolved. The Constitution had also counted slaves as three-fifths of a person, which gave the Southern states a decided advantage in Congress before the war.

Former slaves, however, would now be whole persons, which could further skew Congressional representation–unless the former slaves could vote. The year 1865 saw the end of armed conflict as well as the end of wartime reconstruction. In March 1865, Congress had passed the Freedmen's Bill, establishing the Bureau of Refugees, Freedmen and Abandoned Lands. Also that year, the Thirteenth Amendment to the U.S. Constitution had been proposed and swiftly ratified, legally abolishing slavery in the United States. Andrew Johnson became president that year, after the assassination of President Lincoln, and tried to declare that the war's objective (restoration of the Union) had been achieved. In December 1865, the 39th Congress of the United States convened, with a solid Republican majority that reflected a powerful shift in how government was expected to function. They were not inclined to agree with the President's desire to call the war won and stand by while the Southern states curtailed the political influence of those formerly enslaved.

Before the Civil War, centralized power had been very much feared. The initial ten amendments to the Constitution, the Bill of Rights, had specified a great many things that Congress was not to do. The politics of the day was to limit centralized power. Andrew Jackson had deliberately crippled the National Bank of the United States, not really understanding the need or benefits of a modern nation having a solid fiscal foundation. Nullification of federal laws had also been debated and even attempted. Centralized authority, however, had now won a war and finally overcome the slave power that had dominated American politics since the Revolution. The amendments that emerged from the Civil War, beginning with the Thirteenth, made clear that Congress might be constrained in some instances, but could act strongly in other instances.

A tension developed between Congress, which was trying to solidify the results of the Civil War, and President Johnson, who simply wanted to call the war over. The immediate issue was that Southern states had begun to criminalize joblessness, homelessness, and other conditions experienced by persons formerly enslaved. These new laws were meant to exert control over the critically needed labor force. Congress, however, was not willing to see the Southern aristocracy reestablish its hegemony and reclaim control of the federal legislature. The Congressional Republicans began a new effort to push beyond the relatively benign reconstruction that had been expedient during the war and to address these emerging issues.

Early in 1866, Congress voted to extend the Freedmen's Bill, having to overrode President Johnson's veto to do so. In April, Congress passed a Civil Rights Act, which gave meaning to the Thirteenth Amendment by establishing a national citizenship, whose fundamental rights could not be deprived by state laws. Anticipating legal challenges to a decidedly unfriendly Supreme Court, Congress proposed a Fourteenth Amendment, which finally overruled the Supreme Court's Dred Scott decision that had claimed that black persons were not citizens, but property. The equal protection clause of this new amendment would become the basis of the Civil Rights Act of 1964 and the Voting Rights Act of 1965, but that was far in the future. At the time, the Fourteenth Amendment established the constitutionality of the Civil Rights Act of 1866 through recognition of national citizenship.[1]

In 1866, Fredericksburg's elections for the Town Council proceeded as they always had, comfortably male and white. As Congress increasingly tinkered with the old social order though, riots broke out in some of the larger Southern cities such as Memphis and New Orleans. Disaffected former Confederates murdered former slaves who had the temerity to think they might be citizens. In Virginia, on January 9, 1867, the General Assembly considered the newly passed Fourteenth Amendment and voted to reject rather than ratify it. Congress responded to the growing violence by passing the Reconstruction Act of 1867, again having to override a presidential veto. This Act effectively established martial law in the South so the U.S. Army could protect life and property and supervise local governments. The politics of civil war do not conveniently end when armed conflict does and this new state of affairs is evident in the Council minutes for the election of 1867.

There are two handwritten versions of the Council minutes from this period. There is the record copy, which was written smooth into large, leather-bound volumes. These handsome books provided the basis for the typescripts developed by folks working for the Works Progress Administration during the 1930s. The output from this Depression-era jobs program has been very useful to both local government officials as well as local historians, but these minutes published by the CVBT also include missing words and paragraphs contained in the rough drafts of the minutes and lost in the transition from rough to smooth copies. Any missing portions are enclosed in brackets, to differentiate the few variations between the rough draft and the record copy.

1866

At a Called Meeting of the Common Council of the Town of Fredericksburg, held at the Council Chamber on Friday evening the 19th day of January 1866.

Present–M. Slaughter, Mayor
        J.W. Sener, Recorder

Thomas F. Knox, W[illia]m. A. Little, W.H. Cunningham, Cha[rle]s. Scott, B[everly].T. Gill, James McGuire, Rob[er]t. W. Adams.

Geo[rge]. W. Shepherd elected a member of the Council appeared was qualified and took his seat.

An a/c of A. Walker for pulling down the walls of the Farmers Hotel building amounting to $19.50 is allowed & ordered to be paid. [2]

The Mayor submitted a report in writing of his interview with Mr. A.K. Phillips, in relation to the interests of the Corporation under the will of the late Mrs. Margaret Phillips, which was read and ordered to be filed.

Present–J[ohn].G Hurkamp

The Mayor submitted a communication in writing to the Council touching various subject of interest to the Corporation.

On motion made & seconded, Ordered that the Mayor be instructed to employ four competent men to act as night policemen, upon the best terms he can & report to the Council.

On motion [made] & seconded, Ordered that the Pumps Committee proceed without delay to have all the Public pumps of value in the Corporation, put in complete order.

On the recommendation of the Mayor, It was resolved that a Board of health to consist of three Physicians be appointed for this Corporation, whereupon on motion the Council proceeded to ballot for the members of the board, when Dr. Geo. F. Carmichael, Dr. J.G[ordon]. Wallace & Dr. W[m].S. Scott were duly elected a Board of health for this Corporation, who were respectfully requested to make suggestions and recommendations from time to time to the Council as they may deem expedient and proper in relation to the sanitary condition of the Town.[3]

On motion made & seconded, & in pursuance of the Mayor's recommendation, Ordered that the overseers of the poor be directed to contract with some person for the delivery of thirty cords of wood to be distributed by them in their discretion among the poor of the town.

On motion, Ordered that the discount of five per cent to tax payers be allowed to all who pay their taxes within twenty days after notice that the Commissioners books are in the hands of the Collector, and that the discount of two per cent be allowed to all who pay their taxes within forty days after said notice, and that the Collector be directed to publish said notice as soon as the Commissioners Books are placed in his hands by the Commissioner of the Revenue.

On motion made, Ordered that the Mayor be instructed to confer with the Surveyor of the Corporation and ascertain what it would cost to make a new map or plat of the Town on Parchment and report to the Council.

Mr. Wm. H. Cunningham submitted the following resolution–

Resolved that the Contract made by Mr. Peter Goolrick with Messrs. Little & Goolrick for the prosecution of the claim against the Old Dominion Steam Boat Company at a contingent fee for the amount of the recovery be confirm (sic), and moved that the rules be suspended in order to consider said resolution, which motion was lost.[4]

On motion, the Council Adjd.

M. Slaughter, Mayor

At a Called Meeting of the Common Council of the Town of Fredericksburg, held at the Council Chamber on Friday the 2nd day February 1866.

Present –M. Slaughter, Mayor
J.W. Sener, Recorder
W[illiam].H. Cunningham, B[everly].T. Gill, Ch[arle]s. S. Scott, John J. Young, James McGuire, Geo[rge]. W. Shepherd, George Gravatt.

The Mayor submitted a report in writing of his interview with Col. Ames commanding this post in relation to the delivery of the Jail to the Civil Authorities of this Corporation, Whereupon–

On motion made & seconded, Ordered that the Public property committee be instructed to have the Jail of this Corporation repaired & put in safe & comfortable condition for the reception of Prisoners.

Present–Thomas F. Knox
   "   John G. Hurkamp

Mr. Knox moved that the compensation of the night Police men be fixed at the sum of $50. per month for one to act as Chief of Police, &

The old town hall had been built in 1816 and remained in continuous use until 1984.

$40 per month for the remaining three, which motion Mr. Scott moved to lay on the table, which was carried.

Mr. Scott moved to reconsider the action of the last meeting instructing the Mayor to employ five night Police men, which motion was carried, six members voting in the affirmative.

On motion made & seconded, Ordered that the Public property committee be instructed to wait again upon the Commandant of this post and request the removal of troops now quartered in the Town Hall Building.

A communication from Mr. Julient Perry to the Mayor, was read & on motion, Ordered to be laid on the Table.

On motion the Council Adjd.

M. Slaughter, Mayor

At a Called meeting of the Common Council of the Town of Fredericksburg held at the Council Chamber on Thursday evening, the 15th day of February 1866

Present–M. Slaughter, Mayor
          Joseph W. Sener, Recorder
William A. Little, John G. Hurkamp, John J. Young, Ch[arle]s. S. Scott, B[everly].T. Gill & Geo[rge]. Gravatt.

On motion made & seconded, Ordered that the compensation of the Commissioner of Streets be fixed at one dollar per day whilst he is actually employed in the discharge of his duties.

The Council proceeded to elect by ballot a Commissioner of Streets for this Corporation, when Geo[rge]. Aler was duly elected.

Doctors Carmichael & Wallace declined to act as members of the Board of Health, Whereupon the Council proceeded to fill the vacancies when Doctors Jones & Rose were duly elected members of the Board of Health of this Town to supply the vacancies aforesaid.

On motion, Ordered that the "Young men[s] literary society" be allowed to use the Court house hall on the evenings of their meetings.

On motion made & seconded, Resolved that the products of the present tax bill does not admit of the practicability of receiving the past due coupons of the bonds of this Corporation in payment of taxes for the current year.

On motion, Resolved that the Board of Health be requested to consider promptly all matters relating to the sanitary condition of the town, especially the condition of the Marsh and canal on the west of the Town, and report to the Council.[5]

Resolved, That the Fredg. Agricultural Society be authorized to resume possession of the Mercer Square upon the terms and conditions of its former occupation before the war. The design of said society [being] to review its annual meetings and to endeavor to revive the Society and thus promote the interests & prosperity of this section of the State.[6]

Resolved, that the Telegraph Company be directed to place their post not at Mr. Carters door, but at Wellford's Corner.

On motion, Ordered that James B. Sener, John J. Young & B[everly].T. Gill have permission to plant trees in front of their residences, provided they are not Alanthus (sic) trees, the Street Committee to superintend & point out the location of the trees.[7]

On motion, the Council Adjd.

                                        M. Slaughter, Mayor

At a Meeting of the Common Council of the Town of Fredericksburg, held at the Council Chamber on Friday evening, the 16th day of February 1866.

Present–M. Slaughter, Mayor

J.W. Sener, Recorder

Thomas F. Knox, Charles Scott, B[everly].T. Gill, Geo. Gravatt, John J. Young, John G. Hurkamp, James McGuire,

Common Councilmen.

The Mayor stated that the Council had been convened at the instance & request of three members, to consider some matters connected with the American Telegraph Company.

On motion made & seconded, the action of the Council at the last meeting in relation to the American Telegraph Company was reconsidered.

Mr. Young moved that the order made at the last meeting requiring the American Telegraph Co. to place their post at Wellfords Corner instead of in front of Mr. Carters house, be rescinded. Mr. Scott moved to amend the resolution by appointing a special Committee to consider the whole subject and act definitively thereon. The amendment was lost, whereupon the question occurring on the original resolution the same was carried. Messrs. Sener, Hurkamp & Gravatt, members of the Street Committee was [were] excused from voting on the resolution & amendment.[8]

On motion, Resolved that Street Committee be requested to cause the post of the American Telegraph Company to be placed at Wellfords Corner if practicable to do so, if not, [that] the post remain where it is at present in front of Mr. E. Carter's house. Messrs. Sener, Hurkamp and Gravatt, were excused from voting on this resolution.

Mr. James B. Sener by note in writing, resigned his position as Commissioner of the Freedmens Court, which resignation was accepted.[9]

On motion, the Council Adjd.

M. Slaughter, Mayor

At a Called Meeting of the Common Council of the Town of Fredericksburg held at the Council Chamber on Tuesday the 20th [day of] February 1866.

Present– M. Slaughter, Mayor

J.W. Sener, Recorder

The old jail is still evident in the alley behind the old court house, but also shows various expansions over the years. The door has been replaced by a vent. The area is still called the Jail Alley.

William A. Little, Geo[rge]. Gravatt, John J. Young, Jas. McGuire, John G. Hurkamp, & Thomas F. Knox.

The Mayor stated that he had convened the Council for the purpose of communicating the result of his efforts to procure a suitable person to act for the Citizens as a Comnr. of the Freedmans Court, stated that Mr. W.P. Conway will if desired act as Comnr.

On [motion,] Mr. W.P. Conway was duly elected a Commissioner on the part of the Citizens of the Town in the Freedmans Court.

An a/c of R[obt].W. Hart amounting to $11.64 was presented and ordered to be paid.

On motion made & seconded Joseph W. Sener has permission of leading a branch pipe from the main on the corner of Caroline & George Street & leading into the well at the East corner of said street, for the purpose of cleaning out the water pipes, when it may be deemed advisable to do so.

Resolved, that the Clerk of the Council be instructed to prepare an ordinance repealing all the Corporation laws on the Statute book of the Corporation, relating to slaves.[10]

Resolved, that it is not in the power of the Council to pay the interest on our Corporation debt this year, that the Clerk be instructed under the supervision of the Finance Committee to prepare an ordinance providing for the funding of all the interest now due and accruing during the present year upon the bonds of the Corporation.

On motion, the Council Adjd.

M. Slaughter, Mayor

At a Called Meeting of the Common Council of the Town of Fredericksburg held at the Council Chamber on Friday evening the 2nd day of March 1866.

Present– M. Slaughter, Mayor
        J[oseph].W. Sener, Recorder
W[illiam].A. Little, W.H. Cunningham, John J. Young, G.W. Shepherd, B[everly].T. Gill, John G. Hurkamp, Robt. W. Adams, James McGuire, Ch[arle]s. S. Scott, Thomas F. Knox.

The Mayor stated that the Council had been convened for the purpose of considering various matters of interest to the Town.

It appearing by [the] survey made by Carter M. Braxton, Civil Engineer, that in order to drain the Marsh through Kenmore & Sandy Bottom, a sufficient fall cannot be obtained without leaving the culverts constructed by the Rail Road Company near the Depot. It is ordered that the Mayor inform the Richmond Fredg. & Potomac Railroad Company, that the Council desires that said Company shall make the needful alteration of said culvert as speedily as practicable, in order that the same may be completed while the work of draining said Marsh is progressing, And [that] the Council declining the removal of such an obstruction as called for by the time of the original agreement made by said Company in obtaining the right-of-way through the Town, asks for a prompt cooperation by said Company in this matter, which is deemed important to the health of the Town.

On motion, ordered that John B. Alexander, H[arry].B. Hermes, L.J. Huffman & Ch[arle]s. S. Scott, be severally summoned to appear forthwith before this Council to give evidence &c.

On motion made & seconded, Ordered that a Committee to consist of four members be appointed to take into consideration all matters connected with the draining of the Marsh on the West of the Town, and to confer with John L. Marye, Esqr. and all persons interested therein, and to report this action to the adjourned meeting of the Council on Tuesday evening next.[11]

The Mayor appointed the following Committee under the foregoing resolution, Viz. Charles S. Scott, James W. Sener, Wm. A. Little & Wm. H. Cunningham.

A Report from the Street Committee was presented & ordered to be laid on the table by the following vote, Yeas–Knox, Little, Cunningham, Adams, McGuire, Gill, Noes–Hurkamp, Sener, Young & Shepherd.

On motion, Resolved, that Col. Braxton Engineer for the Rail Road Company be requested to proceed as speedily as possible to do the further work up [on] the streets of the Town, as suggested by the report of the Street Committee. The yeas & nays were demanded upon this resolution, and resulted as follows–Yeas Messrs. Knox, Little, Cunningham, Adams, Scott, Shepherd, McGuire & Gill, Nays–Messrs. Hurkamp, Sener & Young.

On motion, the Petition of John L. Knight, Jr. & other Citizens was referred to the Street Committee for their action.

On motion, Resolved that the sum of $500 be appropriated to the purchase of Fire apparatus for this Corporation, and that the agents of the Insurance Companies & private citizens of the Town be requested to aid as far as possible by their contribution in effecting this very desirable work. Said appropriation not to be used until enough money has been raised to purchase an Engine, of eight-inch cylinders & seven hundred feet of Hose for said purpose & that the Commander of the Fire Company be requested to solicit subscriptions to carry out the above object.

On motion, the Council Adjd.

M. Slaughter, Mayor

At an adjd. meeting of the Common Council of the Town of Fredericksburg, held at the Council Chamber on Tuesday evening the 6th March 1866.

Present– M. Slaughter, Mayor
   J[oseph].W. Sener, Recorder
Thomas F. Knox, W[illia]m. A. Little, George Gravatt, Wm. H. Cunningham, John G. Hurkamp, John J. Young, G[eo].W. Shepherd,

B[everly].T. Gill, Charles S. Scott, James McGuire, R[obert].W. Adams.

The Committee appointed on Friday last to consider all matters connected with the draining of the Kenmore Marsh submitted a report of their action, in the premises, whereupon a motion was made & seconded the report of the Committee was approved & adopted.

Mr. Little offered the following resolution, Resolved that the sum of $ be appropriated for the purpose of draining the Kenmore Marsh & the Valley on the West of the town, from said Marsh to the Richmond, [and] Fredsburg Rail Road, to be expended by a Committee appointed by the Council, consisting of one member of the Kenmore Company, one of the Water Power Company, & two appointed by this body, which appropriation together with $500 tendered for this purpose by the Kenmore & Water Power Company, deemed sufficient for such purpose.

2d. That said Committee be instructed to contract as soon as possible under the supervision of a competent Engineer, with some responsible party to said work speedily and thoroughly.

3d. That John E. Tackett, on the part of the Water Power Company, John L. Marye on the part of the Kenmore Company, & M. Slaughter, Mayor & W.S. Scott, President of the board of Health constituted said Committee, which on motion made & seconded was ordered to be laid on the Table.

On motion made & seconded, Ordered that a committee be appointed to carry out the report of the Committee in relation to draining the Kenmore Marsh.[12]

On motion, Ordered that said Committee consist of three members & Messrs. John E. Tackett, Ch[arle]s. S. Scott & John G. Hurkamp were duly appointed said Committee.

On motion, Ordered that the sum of $200. be appropriated for the purpose of carrying out the recommendation of the Special Committee in relation to draying (sic) [draining] the Kenmore Marsh.

On Motion, the Council Adjd.

            M. Slaughter, Mayor

At a Called Meeting of the Common Council of the Town of Fredsburg, held at the Council Chamber on thursday evening the 15th March, 1866.

Present–M. Slaughter, Mayor

J[oseph].W. Sener, Recorder

W[illia]m. A. Little, John J. Young, John G. Hurkamp, Charles Scott, James McGuire, George Gravatt, W[illia]m. H. Cunningham, B[everly].T. Gill & Thomas F. Knox.

The Mayor having made a favorable report, ordered that the Chamb[erlai]n. pay to the Police officers their salaries for the Quarter ending the 19th inst.

The following accounts were read, passed and ordered to be paid:

James McGuire	$2.00
J.W[illiam]. Adams	5.00
New Era, Office	16.50
Fredericksburg "Ledger"	24.75
Virginia Herald	18.00
J.J. Chew	7.76
Scott & Bowering	18.30
M. Slaughter	22.00

On Motion, Ordered that the bill presented by Lewis O. Magrath amtg. to four dollars be laid on the table.

On Motion, Ordered that the Chamberlain pay to Robt. Dignum the sum of ten dollars, amount paid by him to the Federal Military for permission to sell liquor &c.

On Motion, Ordered that one of the Police officers of this Corporation proceed to collect forthwith from Wm. Lange the sum of $18.30 amount of account due to Messrs. Scott & Bowering.

The Special Committee in relation to draining the Kenmore Marsh made a report, whereupon on motion made & seconded the further sum of $150 is appropriated for the purpose of effecting the object of the Committee.

It is hereby certified by the Council, that the Council has not furnished a Mayors office during the past year & the Mayor therefore has been compelled to use his private counting room for that purpose, for which he has charged no rent. Also that no clerk of the Market having been appointed, the ordinances relating to the Market, if not enforced, has not been owing to any want of diligence of the Mayor in that regard.

On motion of Mr. Cunningham permission is granted him to plant trees in front of his house on Caroline Street, under the supervision of the Street Committee.

Resolved, that Mr. John G. Hurkamp be permitted to enclose the unopen street through Alsop's lots near the basin, said enclosure to be removed whenever ordered by the Council.[13]

On Motion, Ordered that the trees planted by Mr. Bradley in front of the Baptist Church remain where they are now planted.

On Motion, Ordered that the report of the Street Committee laid upon the Table at a former meeting, be taken up, and that the same be returned to the Committee.

Ordered that the Sergeant of this Corporation procure a suitable ballot box for this Corporation & the sum of $1.50 is appropriated for that purpose.

On Motion, the Council Adjd.

        M. Slaughter, Mayor

At a Meeting of the Common Council of the Town of Fredericksburg, at the Council Chamber on Saturday evening the 17th day of March 1866.

Present– M. Slaughter, Mayor
    J.W. Sener, Recorder
Ch[arle]s. S. Scott, Geo. Gravatt, James McGuire, John G. Hurkamp, Geo[rge]. W. Shepherd, W[illia]m. A. Little, B[everly].T. Gill,
    Common Councilmen.

The Finance Committee reported that they had examined & adjusted the account of George F. Chew, Chamberlain of the Corporation, [ending] the 17th day of March, 1866, and found the same to be correct and supported by proper Vouchers and a balance due the Corporation by the Chamberlain of Eighty three dollars & twenty cents. The report was received & approved.

The Finance Committee report[ed] that they had examined the account of L[andon].J. Huffman, Collector of Taxes for the Corporation of Fredericksburg, and found [find] the same to be correct & showing a balance of $3461.17 of uncollected taxes in the hands of the Collector. The report was received and approved.

On Motion, the Council Adj[ourne]d.

        M. Slaughter, Mayor

At an Adjourned Meeting of the Common Council of the Town of Fredericksburg, on Monday March 19th, 1866.

Present– M. Slaughter, Mayor

J.W. Sener, Recorder

William A. Little, Geo[rge]. Gravatt, Ch[rle]s. S. Scott, B[everly].T. Gill, John G. Hurkamp, William H. Cunningham, James McGuire, Thomas F. Knox, John J. Young, Common Councilmen.

This being the day fixed by law for the election of twelve men to serve as Common Councilmen of the Town of Fredericksburg, until the third Monday in March next 1867, and until others are elected in their stead, the voters met at the Clerk's Office in the Court House of said Corporation and deposited their ballots, and after counting the same, it was found that the largest number votes were given for the following persons, to wit— George Gravatt 315, John G. Hurkamp 289, John E. Tackett 278, W[illia]m. H. Cunningham 253, Thomas F. Knox 245, E.M. Braxton 237, W[illia]m. A. Little 229, John J. Young 225, James McGuire 197, A[bsalom].P. Rowe 157, James H. Bradley 138, George W. Wroten 134, J[oseph].W. Sener 115, A[ndrew].B. Adams 85, G[eorge].W. Shepherd 84, C. Armat 67, B.F. Bowering 65, Ch[arle]s. S. Scott 64, the first named twelve of whom were declared duly elected.[14]

On Motion, the Council adjourned.

M. Slaughter, Mayor

Council Chamber
Fredericksburg, March 20th,

George Gravatt, John E. Tackett, W[illia]m. H. Cunningham, Thomas F. Knox, E.B.[M.] Braxton, W[illia]m. A. Little, A[bsalom].P. Rowe, James H. Bradley, Geo[rge]. W. Wroten, James McGuire, John James Young, & John G. Hurkamp,

Common Councilmen.

Members elect of the Common Council of the Town of Fredericksburg, met at the Council Chamber and severally took the oaths of office before M. Slaughter, Esq., Mayor of the Corporation.

On Motion, Thomas F. Knox was called to the Chair and John James Chew was appointed Clerk pro tem.

On motion, the salary of the Mayor was fixed at $400 to the third Monday in March next.

The Council then proceeded to the election of a Mayor for [of] this Corporation, when Montgomery Slaughter, Esq. unanimously elected, and took the several oaths of office before J.G[ordon]. Wallace, a Justice of the Peace for the Corporation of Fredericksburg and took his seat at the Board.

On motion made, the Salary of the Clerk of the Council was fixed at two dollars per session.

George F. Chew, was duly elected Clerk of the Council.

Thomas F. Knox was elected Recorder of the Corporation and took the several oaths of office before M. Slaughter, Mayor of the Corporation of Fredericksburg.

The Salaries of the following officers were fixed as follows:

The Chamberlain of the Corporation, three hundred dollars.

The Com[missione]r. of the Revenue, two hundred & fifty dollars.

The Collector of Taxes & Rents, 2 per cent on all taxes collected by [to] the day of & 5 per cent on taxes recd. thereafter & 2 per cent on rents.

The Superintendent of Streets, one hundred dollars.

The Clerk of the Market, one hundred dollars.

The Council then proceeded to the election of officers for the current year, when Geo[rge]. F. Chew was elected Chamberlain of the Corporation.

Rob[er]t. W. Hart–Commissioner of the Revenue.

Landon J. Huffman–Collector of Taxes & Rents.

Carter M. Braxton–was elected Surveyor.

Charles Bragdon–was elected Inspector & Measurer of Lumber, wood &c.

John M. Edington, was elected Weigher & Measurer of Coal, Grain, Salt, &c.

George Aler–Superintendent of Streets.

On motion, the number of Police officers for the current year was fixed at two, and their Salaries were fixed at $200. each per annum.

The Council then proceeded to elect Police officers for the current year, when James A. Taylor & John S.G. Timberlake were elected.

The Mayor appointed the following standing Committees, Viz:

On Finance–W[illia]m. A. Little, Wm. H. Cunningham & J.H. Bradley.

On Public Property–James McGuire, E.M. Braxton & Geo. W. Wroten.

On Streets–John G. Hurkamp, Jno. E. Tackett & Geo. Gravatt.

On Pumps–Thomas F. Knox, Jno. J. Young & A.P. Rowe.

Richard Caldwell was elected Clerk of the Market.

Mr. Cunningham moved that the Collector of Taxes be allowed the sum of 7 ½ per cent upon the uncollected taxes [in his hand]. Mr. McGuire moved to amend the motion by making the allowance ten per cent to the Collector, the amendment was lost and the original motion adopted, fixing the compensation of the Collector at seven & a half per cent, upon the uncollected taxes of the last year in his hands.

The tax on Drays, Carts & Wagons for the present year was fixed as follows, Viz: On Drays & Carts five dollars and on Wagons ten dollars.[15]

James A. Taylor, John S.G. Timberlake, Geo[rge]. Aler, Richard Caldwell & John M. Edington, took the oath of office before the Mayor of this Corporation.

On motion, permission is granted the Trustees of [the] Presbyterian Church to plant trees around their church under the supervision of the Street committee.

On motion, permission is granted Mr. Edwin Carter to plant trees in front of his house on Caroline Street, under the supervision of the Street Committee.

On motion, the Council Adj[ourne]d.

M. Slaughter, Mayor

At a Called Meeting of the Common Council of the Town of Fredericksburg, at the Council Chamber on Thursday the 23d day of March, 1866.

Present– M. Slaughter, Mayor
Thomas F. Knox, Recorder
John G. Hurkamp, A.P. Rowe, Wm. H. Cunningham, G[eorge].W. Wroten, E.M. Braxton, John E. Tackett, Jas. H. Bradley, John J. Young, James McGuire,
Common Councilmen.

On motion, Mr. James Chew was [is] appointed Clerk pro tem.

The official bond of Geo. F. Chew, as Chamberlain of this Corporation in the penalty of ten thousand dollars, with John James Chew, Rob[er]t. S. Chew & John G. Hurkamp as securities, was presented to the board, approved and ordered to be filed with the [Mayor] to be by him deposited by him in the National Bank of Fredericksburg for safe keeping.

On motion, Ordered that the Committee on the Market be requested to call upon the owners of the Kenmore property for the sum of $300, promised by them towards the reclamation of the Marsh on the West of the Town.

On motion of Mr. Tackett, Resolved that the Mayor be requested on behalf of the Corporation to notify the Kenmore Company & all of their property holders that they must immediately drain the marshes on their property & on failure on their part the Corporation shall proceed to drain the property and assess the amount to said Company or [&] other property holders.

Absalom P. Rowe was appointed a member of the Committee on the Marsh in the stead of Charles S. Scott.

On motion of Mr. Tackett, Resolved that the sum of one hundred & fifty dollars be appropriated to the completion of the Drainage of the Kenmore Marsh, and the Finance Committee are hereby authorized to borrow the amount if necessary.

On motion, Ordered that the Public property committee be requested to provide a suitable office for the use of the Mayor & also for the meeting of the Council.

On motion, Ordered that all persons engaged or doing business in any Gift Enterprise in this Corporation be required to pay a tax of one hundred dollars per month or for a less period.

Mr. Geo[rge]. Gravatt by note in writing addressed to the Council resigned his seat as a member of the board, which resignation was on motion received.

The Council then proceeded to elect a member to supply the vacancy occasioned by the resignation of Mr. Geo. Gravatt, when Mr. J.W. Sener was elected on the first ballot.

The Official bond of Mr. L.J. Huffman as Collector of Taxes in the penalty of $10,000 with W.P. Conway & Securities, was presented to the board & approved & ordered to be filed with the Mayor to be by him deposited in the National Bank of Fredericksburg for safe keeping.

On motion, Ordered that L.B. Doggett be allowed to obtain a license to conduct business by paying a pro rata tax.

A Bill of Morrison & Beall amounting to nine dollars was presented & ordered to be paid.

A.P. Rowe, Esq. was appointed a member of the Committee on Streets in the place of Mr. Gravatt resigned.

On motion, the Council Adjd.

            M. Slaughter, Mayor

At a Meeting of the Common Council of the Town of Fredericksburg, held at the Council Chamber on Saturday the 24th day of March 1866.
Present– M. Slaughter, Mayor
Thomas F. Knox, Recorder
James McGuire, John E. Tackett, A.P. Rowe, E.[M.] Braxton, Geo[rge]. W. Wroten, Wm. H. Cunningham, Wm.A. Little, John G. Hurkamp, James H. Bradley,
Common Councilmen.

Joseph W. Sener, member of the Council elect, appeared, was qualified before the Mayor & took his seat at the board.

On motion of E.M. Braxton, Resolved that the order of the Council made at the last meeting laying a tax on persons conducting the Gift Enterprise business be reconsidered.

On motion, Resolved that the order made at the last meeting imposing a tax on persons conducting the Gift Enterprise business be and the same is hereby rescinded the Council being of opinion that the said business is a lottery.

R[obert].W. Hart, Commissioner of the Revenue of this Corporation took the oaths of office before the Mayor.

On motion, Resolved, that the ordinance on the subject of scales &c in the Market be amended as follows, that Patent Spring Ballances (sic) may be used by the butchers & others in the Market, subject to the supervision and correction of the Clerk of the Market.

On motion, the Council Adjd.

M. Slaughter, Mayor

At a Called Meeting of the Common Council of the Town of Fredericksburg, held at the Council Chamber on Monday evening the 9th day of April 1866.
Present– M. Slaughter, Mayor
William A. Little, Geo[rge]. W. Wroten, John G. Hurkamp, John E. Tackett, Joseph W. Sener, John J. Young & James H. Bradley, A[bsalom].P. Rowe, William H. Cunningham,
Common Councilmen.

The Mayor stated that he had convened the Council at the request of the Marsh Committee.

On motion of Mr. John E. Tackett, Ordered that the third section of Chapter 38, subject of nuisances be amended & reenacted [so] as to read as follows,

Every person owning or occupying a lot on which there may be a sunken place holding stagnant water, neglecting to fill up or drain the same, or to commence said work within three days after notice to do so, by a Police officer, & continue steadily to do said work, shall forfeit & pay not less than five dollars nor more than ten dollars for every day after the service of said notice, if he shall continue in default, and shall neglect to fill up such place or drain the same.

On motion, Ordered that F.T. Miller, be allowed a credit on his license for a Daguerian Gallery for the next year of ten dollars.[16]

On motion, Ordered that the Commissioner of the Revenue grant a license to W.U. Dillard & Lewis Kueger for the unexpired time of one month, provided said Dillard & Kueger renew their licenses for the next year.

On motion, Ordered that Mr. A.P. Rowe, be permitted to use Mr. Francis old shops as a Soap & Candle Factory during the pleasure of the Council.

On motion, the Council Adjourned.

M. Slaughter, Mayor

At a Called Meeting of the Common Council held at the Council Chamber, May 3rd 1866.

Present– M. Slaughter, Mayor
E.M. Braxton, John E. Tackett, Ja[me]s. H. Bradley, John J. Young, J[oseph].W. Sener, Geo. W. Wroten & A.P. Rowe,
        Common Councilmen.

On motion John J. Young was appointed Clerk Pro-tem.

The Mayor presented a written communication announcing the death of Geo[rge]. F. Chew, Clerk of the Council and Chamberlain of the Corporation, which on motion, was ordered to be filed and recorded, Viz:
Mayor's Office
Fredericksburg May 3rd 1866,

To the Common Council
"Gentlemen, It is my sad duty to announce to you the death of Geo[rge].

F. Chew, Esq., the accomplished and efficient Clerk of the Council and Chamberlain of the Corporation. In communicating this melancholy event I cannot refrain from saying a few words in token of my appreciation of his character as a faithful officer and valued citizen. For many years our official duties brought us into daily intercourse, it was therefore my fortune, to know him intimately. Possessed of rare abilities, remarkable accuracy, and familiarity with all matters pertaining to the history and interests of the Corporation, he was ever at his post, prompt to discharge the obligations of his office, and to meet the constant demands upon him for gratuitous labor & information. His intelligence, skill and fidelity as an officer, commanded the confidence and admiration of his associates. His kind disposition, courteous bearing and accommodating spirit, secured the esteem and regard of all who knew him. His loss will be severely felt & sincerely lamented, by the Officers of this Corporation, and by the Community generally. It is for you, Gentlemen of the Council, to determine what action shall be taken by your body, in respect to his memory and remains.

M. Slaughter, Mayor

On motion, it was resolved, That William A. Little, E.M. Braxton and the Mayor be appointed a Committee to draft suitable resolutions for the occasion,

Whereupon the said Committee reported the following resolutions, which were unanimously adopted by the Council and ordered to be placed in its records, to wit:

<u>RESOLVED</u>   That we have received with unfeigned sorrow the intelligence of the death of George F. Chew, Esq., Chamberlain of this Corporation and Clerk of the Council, a citizen and an officer, whose loss cannot be too deeply deplored, and whose place it will be difficult, if not impossible, to supply. During the long years in which many of us have been associated with him as an officer of this Corporation, it gives us pleasure to testify to his uncommon abilities, his accurate and systematic habits of business, and the courtesy and kindness of disposition exhibited by him in all our official and private intercourse and to record the unanimous sentiment of this Body, that the inscrutable Providence which has thus removed him will be as deeply felt in the loss of this invaluable official services, as it is sincerely lamented by us as his fellow Citizens and personal friends. He was an honest and upright man, a useful and valuable Citizen, [a] faithful, experi-

enced and most accomplished officer, and at the termination of a long and useful life, is followed by the unmingled regrets and the unqualified admiration of all with whom he was for so many years associated.

RESOLVED That the Mayor and members of the Council attend the funeral in a body.

On motion, the Council Adjd.

At a Called Meeting of the Common Council of the Town of Fredericksburg held at the Council Chamber on Friday evening the 11th of May 1866.

Present– M. Slaughter, Mayor
William A. Little, Geo[rge]. W. Wroten, John J. Young, E.M. Braxton, Wm. H. Cunningham, James H. Bradley, Absalom P. Rowe,
   Common Councilmen.

A Communication from the Board of health was received, read, and ordered to be filed.

The Mayor presented a communication from Mr. Solan, which on motion was referred to the Street Committee, who are directed with the aid of the Commissioner of Streets to consider the same and report at the next meeting of the Council.

On Motion ordered that the sum of two hundred and eighty five dollars be appropriated, to be expended under the supervision of the Committee this day appointed by the Council of this Corporation in repairs of the Court house.

The Council proceeded to the election of a Clerk of the Council to supply the vacancy occasioned by the death of the late incumbent, whereupon the vote being taken by ballot, R[obert].S. Chew was duly elected.

The Council proceeded to the election of a Chamberlain of this Corporation, whereupon the vote being taken by ballot, R[obert].S. Chew was unanimously elected.

On Motion, Ordered that the Collector of Taxes allow to all persons who paid a Military tax, who have not received the same, a Credit on any future tax bill he may have against such persons, to the extent of the amount of said Military tax so paid by them.

Ordered that Chap. 35, Section 1, of the Corporation laws be amended by the insertion of the words other "Vehicles" after the words dray carts & wagons.

Ordered that the Tax on vehicles drawn by one horse be fixed at five dollars and on vehicles by two horses at ten dollars.

The finance committee reported that they had examined and adjusted the accounts of Geo[rge]. F. Chew, late Chamberlain of this Corporation ending the 2nd day of May 1866, and found the same to be correct & supported by proper vouchers & a balance due to the Corporation by the late Chamberlain of $91.71. The report was received & approved and the balance ordered to be paid over to the Chamberlain elect, upon his qualification.

Rob[er]t. S. Chew, elected Clerk of the Council and Chamberlain of the Corporation, appeared, and took the oaths of office before the Mayor.

Resolved, that the uncollected taxes of the year 1862, now in the hands of the Collector be remitted and the Finance Committee be directed to settle the accounts of the Collector for said taxes, according to this resolution.

Resolved that the Mayor be instructed to prepare a petition to be signed by the Council and presented to the proper authorities for permission to levy a Mud tax not to exceed cents per ton upon all vessels entering the port of Fredericksburg, the proceeds of said Tax to be exclusively appropriated to removing the obstructions in the river and deepening and cleaning out the Channel.

And then the Council Adjd.

M. Slaughter, Mayor

At a Called Meeting of the Common Council of the Town of Fredericksburg, held at the Council Chamber on Friday evening, the 8th day of June 1866.

Present– M. Slaughter, Mayor
> Thomas F. Knox, Recorder

James H. Bradley, J.W. Sener, E.M Braxton, W.A. Little, Wm. H. Cunningham, Jno. E. Tackett, James McGuire,
> Common Councilmen.

The Mayor stated that the Council had been convened for the purpose of considering various matters of interest to the Corporation.

The official bond of Robt. S. Chew, as Chamberlain of the Corporation, in the penalty of Ten thousand dollars, with John J. Chew & H.B. Hermes as securities, was presented to the board, approved and ordered to be filed with the Mayor, to be by him deposited in the National

Bank of Fredericksburg for safe keeping.

William A. Little, Thos. F. Knox & James H. Bradley are appointed Proxies to represent the interests of the Corporation in the Fredg. & Gordonsville Rail Road Company at any meeting of the Stockholders of said Company to be held hereafter.

Resolved, that the police officers be directed to serve a notice upon Dr. B.R. Wellford, requiring him to grade & put in order the pavement & footing in front of his house at the Corner of Hanover & Princess Ann (sic) Streets.[17]

The Mayor presented a communication from Mr. C.C. Wellford which on motion was laid on the table.

On Motion, the application of H. Wissner & Co. for a remission of license tax, was laid upon the table.

On Motion made & seconded, all action on the Tax bill is postponed to an adjourned Meeting of the Common Council to be held on Tuesday evening the 12th inst. at 5 o'clock P.M.

On Motion, Ordered that the Public Property Comtee. be authorized to contract with Jesse White to do the Corporation printing in payment of rent of office occupied by him.

On Motion, the Council Adjourned till 5 o'clock P.M. June 12th, 1866.

M. Slaughter, Mayor

At an adjourned meeting of the Common Council of the Town of Fredericksburg held at the Council Chamber on Tuesday June 12th, 1866.

Present– M. Slaughter, Mayor

Thos. F. Knox, Recorder

Wm. A. Little, Wm. H. Cunningham, Jas. H. Bradley, E.M. Braxton, Jno. E. Tackett, James McGuire, John G. Hurkamp, A[b].P. Rowe, Jno. J. Young, J[as].W. Sener & Geo. W. Wroten,

Common Councilmen.

On motion made & seconded the report of the Finance Committee was divided into two sections.

Mr. E.M. Braxton offered the following Resolution,

"Resolved that it is deemed inexpedient to levy any tax to pay any portion of the interest on the Corporation debt at this time"–which being seconded,

The Fredericksburg & Gordonsville Railroad finally opened operations in the 1870s. A modern bicycle/pedestrian trail follows the old rail bed, connecting downtown Fredericksburg with several outlying neighborhoods.

And the ayes and noes being called for the resolution was rejected by the following Vote:
Ayes– Messrs. Bradley, Braxton, McGuire, Rowe & Wroten ……………5
Noes– " Knox, Little, Cunningham,
   Tackett, Hurkamp, Young & Sener……………………………………..7

An ordinance imposing taxes for the Year 1866 was passed and is in the words & figures following, to wit:

1st Be it ordained by the Mayor and Common Council of the Town of Fredericksburg that there shall be levied and collected on persons, property and other subjects of the Town of Fredericksburg to defray the expenses of the Corporation, for the year ending the third Monday in March 1867, the taxes following to wit:

2^{d} On Real Estate fifty cents on every hundred dollars value thereof agreeable to the Commissioner's Books.

3^{d} On Personal property fifty cents on every hundred dollars value thereof agreeable to the Commissioner's Books.

4th On each colored male above the age of twenty one years, Two (2) dollars.[18]

5th On all licenses and other subjects assessed with State taxes within the Corporation of Fredericksburg, (except Brokers which are taxed 25 per cent) 50 per cent of [the] said Tax assessed for this Year by the State of Virginia, and excepting theatrical & other exhibitions which are taxed under an ordinance of the Corporation.

6th And it is further ordered that one fourth of the taxes so assessed by this bill for the Corporation, be received in the interest past due on the bonds of the Corporation of Fredericksburg at par.

 Ordered that the Chamberlain be instructed to renew a lost registered Corporation Bond No. 342 for $100 to [C.] Wistar Wallace after due advertisement & upon his giving the usual bond.

 Ordered, that the Chamberlain be instructed to renew a lost registered Corporation Bond No. 240 for $150 to Jas. B. Ficklen, after due advertisement & upon his giving the usual bond.

 Mr. C.W. Wallace appeared before the Council & permission being granted him, was heard upon a communication of Messrs. Morrison & Beall, which he presented, and on motion the said communication was laid on the table.

A bill of Jesse White amounting to $11.50 for printing for the Corporation, was ordered to be paid.

And then the Council Adj[ourne]d.

          M. Slaughter, Mayor

At a Called Meeting of the Common Council of the Town of Fredericksburg, held at the Council Chamber on Friday the 24th day of August 1866.

Present– M. Slaughter, Mayor [not on roster in draft minutes]
  Thos. F. Knox, Recorder
J.J. Young, J.H. Bradley, Jas. McGuire, J.G. Hurkamp, J.W. Sener, Geo. W. Wroten,
    Common Councilmen.

The Mayor presented a communication from T.B. Barton, Esq., Attorney for the Commonwealth, in regard to the collection of the ground rents due the Corporation by Messrs. J.B. Ficklen and D. Green, Esqr., which on Motion, made and seconded, was referred to the Finance Committee for consideration and final action.

A copy of the report of the Grand Jury, made at July Court last, in regard to the condition of the Corporation jail, was also read by the Mayor, which on Motion made and seconded, was referred to the Public Property Committee, with directions to report at the next meeting of the Council the probable cost of making the needed repairs.

On motion of Mr. J.W. Sener, Ordered that the Street Committee be instructed to call on Jno. L. Marye, Esq., for his contribution of two hundred dollars towards draining the Marsh.

A communication from a committee appointed by the Fredericksburg Fire Co. was also presented, which on motion was laid on the table.

On motion of Mr. J.J. Young ordered that the Collector of Taxes proceed without delay to __?__ for all uncollected taxes due the Corporation for 1865, according to law.

A communication from the Overseers of the Poor was on motion laid on the table.

The following persons were unanimously elected Overseers of the Poor, to serve until the next Annual appointment: Viz: Messrs. James Hayes, Edwin Carter, Edw. L. Heinichen, A.E. Samuel, Wm. Burke and G.W. Wroten.

A communication from Miss Fannie E. Mills was presented and [read,] which on Motion was laid on the table for the present.

A bill of Robert W. Hart, Commissioner of the Revenue for six months services amounting to $125.00 was ordered to be paid.

A bill of Young & Hermes amounting to $9.00 was ordered to be paid.

And then the Council adjourned.

[M. Slaughter, Mayor]

At a Called Meeting of the Common Council of the Town of Fredericksburg held at the Council Chamber on Friday evening August 28th [at 4 ½ o'clock P.M.] 1866

Pres[en]t– M. Slaughter, Mayor
        Thos. F. Knox, Recorder
James McGuire, A.P. Rowe, J.W. Sener, J.G. Hurkamp, Wm. H. Cunningham, Geo. W. Wroten, James H. Bradley, Jno. J. Young,
        Common Councilmen.

The Chairman of the Public Property Committee, Mr. James McGuire, made a verbal report in regard to the Jail, and the repairs necessary to make it secure. The Committee having decided on what repairs should be done, solicited bids for the work, one only being submitted by Mr. Wm. H. Norton, who proposed to do the work in a strong and substantial manner for the sum of $354 20/100, and on motion his bid was accepted, provided the timber used for the wood work shall all be well seasoned, or kiln dried. The work to be executed under the supervision of the Pub. Property Committee, and the same Committee are also authorized to procure suitable locks for the new doors, and as many as may be necessary for the Cell doors.

On Motion made and seconded, Ordered that the Mayor be authorized to employ three additional and competent night policemen for the next sixty days, or longer, if he thinks it necessary, upon the best terms he can and report his action hereon to the next Meeting of the Council.

And then the Council adjourned.

[Thomas F. Knox, Recorder]

At a Called Meeting of the Common Council of the Town of Fredericksburg held at the Council Chamber on Tuesday evening September 4th, 1866.

Present– M. Slaughter, Mayor
Thos. F. Knox, Recorder

Wm. H. Cunningham, E.M. Braxton, J.H. Bradley, J.G. Hurkamp, J.J. Young, J.W. Sener, James McGuire,
Common Councilmen.

A Report in writing was submitted by Messrs. Little and Bradley, of the Finance Committee, in regard to raising money to buy Engine and hose for the Fredericksburg Fire Co., And on Motion, made and seconded, Ordered that a Committee of three of the Council be appointed to act in conjunction with the Committee of the Fire Co. and who are authorized to raise the money upon the terms indicated in the report of the Finance Committee, and also to make purchase of the necessary Engine & Hose, which Engine & Hose are to be [the] property of the Corporation.

The Mayor appointed as the Committee, Messrs. Ja[me]s. H. Bradley, J.G. Hurkamp and J.W. Sener.

The attention of the Council was called to the fixing the compensation & appointment of the Police. On Motion made and seconded, the compensation for the night policemen was fixed at one dollar and fifty cents per night.

[The Mayor respectfully called the attention of the Council to the Ordinance requiring the Council to fix the compensation of the police & to appoint the same.]

On Motion Made and Seconded, the appointment of the three additional night policemen is postponed till Friday evening next at 4 o'clock.

On Motion, Ordered that the Mayor be authorized to give notice by hand bills that the Council would elect three sober and efficient night policemen, on Friday evening, and desiring applicants to submit their claims in writing.

And then the Council adjourned till Friday evening next, September 7th at 4 o'clock [P.M.].

[M. Slaughter, Mayor]

At an adjourned meeting of the Common Council of the Town of Fredericksburg held at the Council Chamber on Friday evening September 7th, 1866

    Present– M. Slaughter, Mayor

        Thos. F. Knox, Recorder

J.W. Sener, A.P. Rowe, W.H. Cunningham, G.W. Wroten, E.M. Braxton, J.H. Bradley, Jas. McGuire, J.G. Hurkamp, J.J. Young,

        Common Councilmen.

A communication from two members of the Board of Health was presented and read by the Mayor recommending the removal of the heavy growth of vegetable matter in the vacant lots, and the Streets of the Town, as being injurious to the health of the Citizens, which on Motion, Made and Seconded, was laid on the table.[19]

The Mayor stated that the next business in order was the election of three night police men, and the following applicants were found to have handed in their names, Viz: B.G. Harris, John Edrington, James A. Cox, Wm. C. Smith, John L. Anderson, John Larkin, C.W. Edrington, Robert C. Hart, M. Cahill, Chas. Shepherd, James L. Cole, Clay Taylor, P. Hedinger, William Gouldman.

After several ballots by the Council, the following named men were elected night policemen–B.G. Harris, Peter Hedinger and John Larkin, to serve during the pleasure of the Council.

The Mayor presented a Communication from Mr. John E. Brophy asking permission to establish a distillery within the Corporate limits of the town, and on Motion, Made and Seconded, the privilege was unanimously granted him.

The Mayor presented a Communication from J.M. Edrington, Measurer of Coal &c asking for an increase in the amount allowed the Measurer for Measuring Coal from twenty five to forty Cents per hundred bushels, which on Motion, Made and Seconded was unanimously laid on the table.

On Motion, Ordered that the Pub. Property Committee be authorized to purchase for the Corporation, Hay & Coal Scales and have them put up at once.

And then the Council adjourned.

                        [M. Slaughter, Mayor]

At a Called Meeting of the Common Council of the Town of Fredericksburg held at the Council Chamber on Thursday September 13th 1866.

Present– M. Slaughter, Mayor

Thos. F. Knox, Recorder

John E. Tackett, E.M. Braxton, Jno. J. Young, J[as].H. Bradley, James McGuire, A.P. Rowe,

Common Councilmen.

On Motion Made and Seconded, Ordered that the Collector of taxes be directed to proceed without delay to collect the Corporation License tax for the present year.

The Mayor stated to the Council that Peter Hedinger, and John Larkin, who were elected two of the night police at the last meeting of the Council, had declined to serve, and the Council proceeded to elect two others in their places, and upon the first ballot, M. Cahill and James L. Cole were elected to serve as night police, during the pleasure of the Council.

The Mayor submitted an application from Mrs. Mary M. Wheeler, asking the remission of a fine of two dollars & fifty cents imposed on her son for firing a gun in the limits of the Corporation, which on Motion Made and Seconded was unanimously laid on the table.[20]

And then the Council adjourned.

[M. Slaughter, Mayor]

At a Called Meeting of the Common Council of the Town of Fredericksburg, held at the Council Chamber on Friday the 21st day of September, 1866.

Present– M. Slaughter, Mayor

E.M. Braxton, J.H. Bradley, Jas. McGuire,

Common Councilmen.

There being no quorum present, the Council stood adjourned.

At a Called Meeting of the Common Council of the Town of Fredericksburg held at the Council Chamber on Wednesday the 26th day of September 1866.

Present– M. Slaughter, Mayor

Thos. F. Knox, Recorder

A.P. Rowe, Geo. W. Wroten, E.M Braxton, Jas. McGuire, Jas. H. Bradley, Wm. H. Cunningham,

Common Councilmen.

The Mayor stated that he had convened the Council for the purpose of considering the laws at present in existence in regard to the disposition of the fines imposed by the Mayor, or to pass some new law in regard to the same.

On Motion, Made and Seconded, Chapter XV of the Ordinances of the Corporation is amended by striking out the words "five dollars" and inserting in place thereof "ten dollars" so as to read "not less that one nor more than ten dollars."

On Motion, Made and Seconded, Ordered, that all fines and penalties imposed since March 20th 1866, or which may be hereafter imposed and collected by the Mayor or other Justice shall be paid over to the Chamberlain quarterly, except where it is otherwise provided by law.

Mr. E.M. Braxton moved that the salary of the police officers be fixed at the sum of three hundred dollars per annum, commencing March 20th 1866, which Mr. W.H. Cunningham moved to amend by inserting two hundred and fifty dollars in lieu of three hundred dollars and being seconded, the question was put and the amendment carried.

The Mayor having reported in writing that the Police Officers had discharged their duties satisfactorily during the last six months, it is ordered that the Chamberlain pay them their salaries for that time.

On Motion, Made and Seconded, Ordered that the salary of the night police be paid weekly, upon the Certificate of the Mayor to the Chamberlain, that they have discharged their duties satisfactorily.

Ordered, that the Public Property [Committee] be instructed to purchase three tons of Coal and a Stove, the latter to be put up in the Mayor's office.

A bill of R.C. Hammack was laid on the table.

On Motion, Made and Seconded, Ordered that all persons arrested hereafter at night for disorderly conduct, or other offences shall be confined in the Corporation jail until the next morning after the arrest, and then to be carried before the Mayor or some other Justice to be dealt with according to law.

And then the Council adjourned.

[M. Slaughter, Mayor]

At a Meeting of the Common Council of the Town of Fredericksburg held at the Council Chamber on Wednesday October 24th 1866.

Present– M. Slaughter, Mayor

Thos. F. Knox, Recorder

Jas. W. Sener, Wm. H. Cunningham, E.M. Braxton, James McGuire, A.P. Rowe, Geo. W. Wroten,

Common Councilmen.

The Mayor stated the Council had been Convened to take into consideration some change in the Ordinance of the Corporation regarding the Charge for weighing on the Corporation Scales.

On Motion of Mr. James McGuire and Seconded, Ordered that Section III, Chapter XII of the Ordinances of the Corporation is amended in this, that the word "three" in the ninth line of said section be stricken out, and the word "five" be inserted in lieu thereof, so as to read "five cents for every nett (sic) hundred pounds thereof.

On Motion of Mr. McGuire, Resolved that the Clerk of the Council prepare an Ordinance requiring that all anthracite coal brought to Town for sale, shall be weighed at the Corporation Scales. This ordinance shall take effect on and after the 3rd Monday in March 1867.

The following bills were read and ordered to be paid:

Fred[bur]g. New Era $15 50/100
Fred[bur]g. Ledger   15 50/100

A bill of W[m].J. Moon for repairing the Town Clock amounting to Seventy five dollars was on motion referred to a Special Committee for investigation.

The Mayor appointed Messrs. E.M. Braxton, W.H. Cunningham and A.P. Rowe as the Committee.

Mr. John E. Tackett, by note in writing addressed to the Council resigned his seat as a member of the Council, which resignation was on Motion accepted.

The Council then proceeded to elect a Member to supply the vacancy occasioned by the resignation of Mr. Jno. E. Tackett, when Mr. J.W. Ford was elected, unanimously, on the first ballot.

And then the Council adjourned.

At a Meeting of the Common Council of the Town of Fredericksburg held at the Council Chamber on Wednesday the 14th day of November 1866.

Present– M. Slaughter, Mayor

   Thos. F. Knox, Recorder

Jas. H. Bradley, Wm. H. Cunningham, Wm. A. Little, E.M. Braxton, J.J. Young, J.G. Hurkamp,

   Common Councilmen.

Mr. James W. Ford, member of the Council elect, appeared, was qualified before the Mayor, and took his seat at the board.

The Special Committee appointed at the last meeting of the Council to consider a claim of Wm. J. Moon for repairing the Town Clock, made a verbal report through Mr. E.M. Braxton, their Chairman, recommending that fifty dollars be paid Mr. Moon in full of all demands to this date against the Corporation, which report was adopted, and fifty dollars ordered to be paid Mr. Moon by the Chamberlain.

On Motion of Mr. J[as].H. Bradley, Ordered that Washington Wright be continued as Clock tender at the rate of Eighteen dollars per annum from this date.

On Motion, Made and Seconded, Ordered that the Mayor be authorized and instructed to assign the interest of the Corporation in the Fredericksburg and Gordonsville Rail Road to Col. C.M. Braxton or his assigns, upon the terms and conditions set forth in the following paper:

"Whereas the General Assembly of Virginia passed an Act on the 10th of January 1866, authorizing the President and Directors of the Fredg. & Gordonsville R.R. Co. to sell the State's interest in the said Road on such terms as a majority of the private stockholders may agree to dispose of their interest in said Road, provided the said Road was completed within five years from the first [day] of January 1866, and the State is released from her subscription to said Road, unpaid. Now therefore We the undersigned [private] stockholders in the Fredericksburg & Gordonsville R. Road Company, in order to induce parties, able to complete said Rail Road, believing its completion would result greatly to their benefit and to the interest of the State, do hereby pledge ourselves and covenant to convey the number of shares of stock written opposite to our respective names, at one cent per share to Col. Carter M. Braxton, or his assigns who shall agree and bind themselves in a manner acceptable to the Board of Directors of the Fred[ericksbur]g. & Gordonsville Rail Road Company, to complete the same upon the conditions named in the said Act of Assembly, whenever a majority of the private Stockholders shall agree and bind themselves in writing to convey their stock in said Rail Road to said party or parties undertaking to complete the same." [21]

On Motion Made & Seconded, Ordered that two fines of one dollar each imposed upon Albert Fortune for driving his wagon on the sidewalk be remitted.

On Motion Made and Seconded, Ordered that Chapter XIX, Section VI be amended by inserting after the word "aforesaid" in the third line, the words "with intent to obstruct said footway."

On Motion Made and Seconded, Ordered that hereafter the Council will meet regularly on the fourth Tuesday in each month at Seven o'clock P.M. and that the Court House bell shall be rung at that hour.

And then the Council adjourned.

[M. Slaughter, Mayor]

At a regular monthly meeting of the Common Council of the Town of Fredericksburg held at the Council Chamber on Tuesday the 27th day of November 1866.

Present– M. Slaughter, Mayor
    Thomas F. Knox, Recorder
Wm. A. Little, Wm. H. Cunningham, Jas. [Joseph] W. Sener, E.M. Braxton, Geo[rge] W. Wroten, John G. Hurkamp, A[bsalom] P. Rowe, Jas. H. Bradley,
    Common Councilmen.

On the application of James L. Cole, night policeman, leave of absence is granted him, to enable him to visit the Country for the benefit of his health.

On motion, E. Dorsey Cole is appointed to act as substitute for James L. Cole during his temporary absence from the Corporation.

Present– John J. Young,
    Common Councilman.

An ordinance for funding the interest due on the bonds of this Corporation was passed in the words following, to wit:

Be it ordained by the Mayor and Common Council of the Town of Fredericksburg that any person to whom interest upon the bonds of the Corporation may be due at the present time, and up to the first day of January 1867, when the amount of interest so due to any such person shall not be less than Fifty dollars, shall be entitled to receive in discharge of such interest, in whole or in part, a bond or bonds of the said Corporation of the date of said first of January 1867, bearing six per cent interest per annum, payable semi-annually, in sums of Fifty dollars or any multiple thereof, the said bonds to be made payable not less than ten years nor more than thirty years after date, as the person receiving them may elect.

On Motion, Ordered that the profit and fees provided for in Chapter XXXIX of the Bye laws of this Corporation, be and they are hereby tendered to any Citizen who will erect and keep up a public Magazine for the keeping of Gun Powder – said building to be located and erected under the supervision of the Public Property Committee.

And then the Council adjourned.

[M. Slaughter, Mayor]

At a Called Meeting of the Common Council of the Town of Fredericksburg held at the Council Chamber on Thursday the 20th day of December 1866.

Present– M. Slaughter, Mayor
Wm. A. Little, Joseph W. Sener, A.P. Rowe, James McGuire, Geo. W. Wroten, Jas. H. Bradley, Jas. W. Ford, John J. Young, Wm. H. Cunningham,

Common Councilmen.

E. Dorsey Cole, appointed at the last meeting of the Council as substitute for James L. Cole, absent by leave of the Council, having resigned his position, On Motion, the Council proceeded to elect a substitute for E. Dorsey Cole, until the return of James L. Cole, George H. Timberlake, Edwd, T. Haynie and C.W. Edrington were put in nomination and a ballot being taken, George H. Timberlake was elected as a night policeman to serve during the temporary absence of Jas. L. Cole.

The Mayor having reported in writing that the Police Officers have discharged their duties during the quarter ending to day, it is ordered that the Chamberlain pay them their salaries for that time.

On Motion, Resolved that the minimum amount of the bonds in which the interest of the Corporation debt to 1st January 1867 is to be funded, be fixed at the sum of Thirty dollars, instead of Fifty dollars, And that the Chamberlain be authorized to issue Certificates of debt for the surplus of interest above thirty dollars or some multiple of thirty dollars in each case, bearing interest at 6 p ct. payable annually and said Certificates to be paid ten years after date, And that the Ordinance passed on the 27th day of November 1866, be amended in conformity with this resolution.

On Motion, Made and Seconded, Ordered that a Committee of three be appointed by the Mayor to ascertain what would be the cost of furnishing lamp posts for lighting the Streets, setting them up, and what would be the Cost of [the] Gas Annually.

The Mayor appointed as the Committee, Messrs. Sener, Bradley and Ford. And then the Council adjourned.

[M. Slaughter, Mayor]

At a Called Meeting of the Common Council of the Town of Fredericksburg, held at the Council Chamber on Thursday the 27th day of December, 1866.

Present– M. Slaughter, Mayor
Geo. W. Wroten, Jas. W. Sener, J.G. Hurkamp, Jas. W. Ford, A.P. Rowe and Thos. F. Knox, Recorder,
    Common Councilmen.
There being no quorum present, the Council stood adjourned.

1867

At a regular meeting of the Common Council of the Town of Fredericksburg held at the Council Chamber on Tuesday the 22nd day of January, 1867.

Present– M. Slaughter, Mayor
    Thos. F. Knox, Recorder

Jas. W. Sener, Wm. A. Little, Jas. H. Bradley, Jas. W. Ford, Geo. W. Wroten, J.G. Hurkamp, Wm. H. Cunningham,
   Common Councilmen.

  The Committee appointed by the Council to ascertain the cost of Fire Engines, Hose &c made a report in writing, and on Motion of Mr. Wm. A. Little, the report of the Committee is adopted and the same Committee is requested to make the necessary purchases of the Engine, Hose & Hose carriage &c, upon the most reasonable terms as to cost and times of payment, not to exceed the statements submitted in said report.

  The Committee appointed by the Council to ascertain what would be the cost of lighting the Streets with gas made a report in writing, which on Motion was laid on the table.

  The Mayor read a communication from the Clerk of the Corporation Court and the Commissioner of the Revenue in regard to the importance of having an accurate map of the town prepared, and also a proposition from C.M. Braxton, Corporation Engineer, proposing to prepare such a map, and on Motion it is ordered that Mr. Braxton be authorized to prepare an accurate map of the Town, upon the terms proposed in his communication.

  The Mayor also presented and read a communication from Mr. Gabl. Johnston asking a remission of part of the tax imposed upon him as an Auctioneer, which on Motion was laid on the table.

  A communication was [also] read from Mrs. Rebecca Sale, asking permission for her hogs to run at large during the winter, which on Motion was laid on the table.

  A bill of J.B. Sener, Editor Fred[sbur]g. Ledger for advertising delinquent list amounting to One Hundred and Seventy three dollars was ordered to be paid.

  A Communication of E.N. Stephens was on Motion laid on the table.

  A bill of Robert W. Hart, Comnr. of the Revenue, amounting to Eighty five 19/100 dollars was ordered to be paid.

  A bill of Johnston & Co. amounting to Eight 38/100 dollars was ordered to be paid.

  On Motion, the resignation of Jas. L. Cole as night police man was accepted.

  Present– James McGuire, Common Councilman.

  On [the] Motion of Mr. J.W. Sener, Resolved that the Committee on Streets be authorized and instructed to notify the owners of the property of the late Alexander Walker, on Wolfe Street, to repair the brick wall now in a dangerous condition, and if not so repaired and rendered safe by the said owners in a reasonable time, then the said Committee are directed to remove the said wall at the expense of the owners to be recovered by warrant.[22]

On motion of Mr. J[as].M. McGuire, permission is granted Capt. C.M. Johnson to plant trees in front of the Union House, under the supervision of the Street Committee.[23]

On motion, Ordered that the Public Property Committee be instructed to have the Engine House repaired and put in proper condition without delay.

And then the Council adjourned.

[M. Slaughter, Mayor]

At a Called Meeting of the Common Council of the Town of Fredericksburg held at the Council Chamber on Wednesday the 23rd day of January 1867.

Present– M. Slaughter, Mayor

Thos. F. Knox, Recorder

Wm. A. Little, A.P. Rowe, Jas. McGuire, J.H. Bradley, J.W. Ford, Wm. H. Cunningham, Geo. W. Wroten, J.W. Sener, J.G. Hurkamp, E.M Braxton, J.J. Young,

Common Councilmen.

The Mayor presented orally a request from Mr. Wm. S. Barton asking that the Council would appoint some one to receive his taxes, he not being willing to settle his account as presented by Mr. Huffman, the regular Collector, which on Motion was laid on the table for the present.

On motion of Mr. Bradley, the bill of Mr. J.B. Sener, Editor Fred[s]burg. Ledger, ordered on last night to be paid was reconsidered.

By consent of the Council Mr. J.B. Sener was heard, when the matter for the present was laid on the table.

Mr. Wm. S. Barton, was by consent of the Council heard, when it was deemed unnecessary to take any steps in the matter, the Ordinances of the Corporation fully covering the case.

Mr. J.W. Sener then moved that the bill of the Editor of the Fred[sbur]g. Ledger, be paid, which was seconded, and was afterwards withdrawn.

On Motion, it was ordered that the sum of Seventy five dollars be paid the Editor of the Fred[sbur]g. Ledger in full of his bill against the

Corporation for printing the delinquent list of real estate.

On Motion of Mr. Wm. A. Little, Resolved that hereafter all printing and publications to be made for this Corporation, shall be made by putting out the same upon the best terms, except so far as the contract at present existing with Mr. Jesse White is concerned, which is not intended to be interfered with hereby.

On Motion, Resolved that the Collector of Taxes be directed to refund to all those persons who have paid him the cost of publishing their taxes in the delinquent list, whenever called on by them.

A bill of Geo. H. Timberlake amounting to Six dollars was ordered to be paid.

On Motion, Resolved that hereafter all bills against the Corporation not certified by the appropriate Committee, be referred to the Finance Committee to be reported upon to the next meeting of the Council.

And then the Council adjourned.

[M. Slaughter, Mayor]

At a regular meeting of the Common Council of the Town of Fredericksburg held at the Council Chamber on Tuesday, the 26th day of February, 1867.

Present–M. Slaughter, Mayor
Wm. A. Little, A.P. Rowe, Jas. W. Sener, Jas. McGuire, J.G. Hurkamp, E.M. Braxton, Jas. W. Ford, Jas. H. Bradley.

The Mayor presented a Communication from sundry Citizens of the town in regard to the old wall and chimney on the Shakespeare lot, And on Motion, the Superintendent of the Streets is ordered to inform the owners that the Council consider the said wall and chimney to be in a dangerous condition and to request that they be pulled down at once.[24]

A communication was also presented from Mr. R. Keyser on behalf of the Mozart Club in regard to renting the upper room of the Town Hall, which on Motion was referred to the Pub. Property Committee, with instructions to ascertain what contract could be made with the said Mozart Club, to report to the next meeting of the Council–generally what should be done in the premises.

A bill of R.F. Knox & Bro. and one of Dr. B.S. Herndon, were referred to the Finance Committee under the order of the Council passed January 23rd, 1867.

A communication from Mr. J.B. Sener, asking a reconsideration by the Council of the vote at the last meeting of the Council allowing him Seventy five dollars in full for his bill for printing the delinquent list of last year, was on Motion laid on the table.

Ordered that the error in the assessment of the income tax charged to Wm. Allen's Estate be corrected and that the Estate be relieved from the payment of $5 04/100, the amount of said error in the tax account for 1866.

A communication was read from Mr. Wm. F. Cheek, which on Motion was referred to the Finance Committee.

Ordered that notice be given by hand bills, to be posted about the town, that a Council of Claims will be held in the Council Chamber on Tuesday, March 12th, 1867.

And then the Council adjourned.

[M. Slaughter, Mayor]

At a Council of Claims held at the Council Chamber on Tuesday the 12th day of March 1867.

Present– M. Slaughter, Mayor
        Thos. F. Knox, Recorder
Jas. W. Sener, Jas. H. Bradley, Wm. A. Little, E.M. Braxton, Geo. W. Wroten, A.P. Rowe, James McGuire, Jas. W. Ford,
        Common Councilmen.

The following bills were read, passed and ordered to be paid:

R.W. Hart amtg. to	$62.50	R.F. Knox & Bro. amtg. to	86c
J.W. Adams " "	$ 8.65	J.H. Kelly " "	$16.00
A.P. Rowe " "	$16.00		

A bill of Doct. B.S. Herndon amounting to $38.00 was reported from the Finance Committee, and on Motion, ordered that the bill be returned to Doctor Herndon with the endorsement of the said Committee, to wit: "The Stay law prevents payment of the above bill just now."

On Motion, ordered that when the Council adjourns, it adjourn to meet on Friday evening the 15th inst. at 7 ½ o'clock.

On Motion, Resolved that Mayor Slaughter be and he is hereby instructed to proceed to Washington City and wait on the President of the

United States and ascertain whether in the approaching municipal election in this Corporation, the right to vote and the qualifications of voters thereby [therein] is to be governed by the Charter of said Corporation, and the existing laws of Virginia, or by the late Act of Congress known as the "Military Bill."[25]

And then the Council adjourned.

[M. Slaughter, Mayor]

At a Called Meeting of the Common Council of the Town of Fredericksburg held at the Council Chamber on Thursday the 14th day of March 1867.

Present–M. Slaughter, Mayor
        Thos. F. Knox, Recorder
Jas. McGuire, A.P. Rowe, Jas. W. Sener, E.M. Braxton, J.H. Bradley, Geo. W. Wroten, Wm. H. Cunningham, Jas. W. Ford and J.J. Young,
        Common Councilmen.

Mayor Slaughter made a verbal report of his visit to Washington City and his interview with the President and the Attorney General of the United States, in accordance with the Resolution of the Council, passed at the last meeting.

On Motion, Resolved that John L. Marye, Jr. be and he is hereby requested to proceed to the City of Richmond, and wait upon Major Genl. Schofield and endeavor to get from him such instructions as shall be a guide to the Commissioners at the approaching Municipal election to be held in the town on Monday next, as to what shall be considered the necessary qualifications of the voters who may present their votes.[26]

On Motion, ordered that the resolution adopted at the last meeting of the Council to meet on Friday evening was reconsidered.

On Motion, ordered that when the Council adjourn, it adjourn to meet on Saturday evening at 4 o'clock.

The Mayor having reported that the Police Officers had discharged their duties satisfactorily during the last quarter, ordered, that the Chamberlain pay them their salaries for that time.

A bill of Wm. S. Barton for costs incurred in the suit of Barton vs. Huffman was ordered to be paid.

And then the Council adjourned till Saturday evening at 4 o'clock.

[M. Slaughter, Mayor]

At a Meeting of the Common Council of the Town of Fredericksburg held at the Council Chamber on Saturday the 16th March 1867.
Present– M. Slaughter, Mayor
    Thomas F. Knox, Recorder
Willm. A. Little, A.P. Rowe, Jas. McGuire, J.G. Hurkamp, Jos. W. Sener, Jas. H. Bradley, Wm. H. Cunningham
    Common Councilmen.

The Finance Committee reported that they had examined and adjusted the account of R.S. Chew, Chamberlain of the Corporation ending the 16th day of March 1867 and found the same to be correct and supported by proper vouchers, and a balance due the Corporation by the Chamberlain of the sum of Four hundred and twenty five [four] 84/100 dollars. The Committee also report that they counted and examined coupons of the bonds of the Corporation, which had been funded by the Chamberlain in accordance with an order of the Council passed December 20th, 1867, amounting to the sum of $4098 00/100 which said coupons have been destroyed by us. The report was received and approved.

The Finance Committee also reported that they had adjusted the account of L.J. Huffman, Collector of taxes &c for the year 1865 and find a balance due by Mr. Huffman of $556.87/100. By direction of the Committee [Mr. Huffman] has given his receipt for that amount, said receipt to be credited from time to time to him, hereafter as the Collector may pay over to the Chamberlain on that a/c.

The Finance Committee also reported that they had examined the account of L.J. Huffman, Collector of Taxes for the year 1866, and find the same to be correct and showing a balance of $6,033 19/100 of uncollected taxes in the hands of the Collector. The report was received and approved.

The Mayor presented a communication from Major Genl. Schofield in the words following to wit:

"Headquarters 1st District State of Va.
Richmond, Va., March 16th, 1867.
Major James Johnson, V.R.C.
Supt. Bureau RF&AL

First—The Municipal election in the City of Fredericksburg which the Charter of that City directs to be held on Monday the 18th inst., is hereby ordered to be suspended until the necessary preparations can be made to fully and fairly execute the provisions of the Act of Congress of March 2nd 1867, concerning the election franchise and qualifications for office. Second – Major James Johnson V.R.C. Supt. Bureau R.F. & A.L. at Fredericksburg will furnish an official copy of this order to the Mayor of the City and one to each of the Civil officers whose duties in connection with the City election are suspended by this order.[27]

By command of Major Genl. Schofield,

       L.F. Chablin, Asst. Adj. Genl.

On Motion the following preamble and resolution was passed: Whereas by an Order this day received from Major Genl. J.M. Schofield, Commanding District No. 1, the State of Virginia, the annual Municipal election, which according to the requirements of the Charter should take place on Monday the 18th day of March 1867, it being the third Monday in said month, is suspended, "until the necessary preparations can be made to fully and fairly execute the provisions of the Act of Congress of March 2nd 1867 by concerning the elective franchise and the qualifications for office.

Therefore, Resolved, By the Mayor and Commonalty of Fredericksburg that in pursuance of said orders the election heretofore advertised to be held on Monday the 18th inst. for Mayor and Common Councilmen, be and it is hereby suspended until further orders.

And whereas further; under Genl. Orders No. 1 issued from the same Head Quarters, all officers under the existing Provisional Government of Virginia, are continued in office for the present, this Council in accordance with said orders hereby resolves, that the persons at present discharging the duties of the offices required by the Charter of this Corporation, be and they are hereby continued in their respective offices until further orders.

Whereas, by an order of the Common Council passed on the 5th day of December 1865, Mr. Thomas B. Barton, was employed as Counsel for the

Corporation [in the case of the Corp.] vs. the Old Dominion Steam Boat Co. and his compensation to be fixed by the Council, resolved that in accordance with that resolution the compensation of Mr. Barton, be fixed at fifty dollars [and that the Chamberlain pay Mr. Barton the sum of fifty dollars] in full of his fee in that case.

And then the Council adjourned.

[M. Slaughter, Mayor]

At a Called Meeting of the Common Council of the Town of Fredericksburg, held at the Council Chamber on Thursday, the 21st day of March 1867.

Present– M. Slaughter, Mayor
Thos. F. Knox, Recorder
Jas. H. Bradley, Jos. W. Sener, Jas. W. Ford, Common Councilmen.

There being no quorum present, the Council stood adjourned.

At a Called Meeting of the Common Council of the Town of Fredericksburg held at the Council Chamber on Friday evening the 22d day of March 1867.

Present– M. Slaughter, Mayor
Thos. F. Knox, Recorder
J.J. Young, E.M. Braxton, J.H. Bradley, James McGuire, Jno. G. Hurkamp, Jas. W. Ford, Jos. W. Sener, Wm. A. Little,
Common Councilmen.

The Mayor stated that the Council had been convened for the purpose of taking into consideration some propositions for clearing the wrecks out of the river and opening the harbor, and [the Mayor] then read a proposition from Saml. Richardson, also one from Wm. J. Marshall.

On motion, Messrs. A.A. Little and John L. Marye, Jr. were heard on the matter under consideration. Mr. Saml. Richardson was also heard.

On Motion, ordered that a committee of three be appointed by the Mayor to confer with the wharf owners and others, to obtain all the information possible on the matter under consideration, to report to the next meeting of the Council.

The Mayor appointed Messrs. J.H. Bradley, E.M. Braxton & Thos. F. Knox, as the Committee.

Ordered, that when the Council adjourns, it adjourn to meet on Monday evening the 25th inst. at 4 o'clock.

Ordered that the License tax on Drays, Carts and Wagons for the year 1867, be fixed at the same rate as for the year 1866.

And then the Council adjourned till Monday at 4 o'clock P.M.

[M. Slaughter, Mayor]

At an adjourned meeting of the Common Council of the Town of Fredericksburg held at the Council Chamber on Monday the 25th day of March 1867, at 4 o'clock P.M.

Present– M. Slaughter, Mayor
   Thos. F. Knox, Recorder
James McGuire, Jos. W. Sener, E.M. Braxton, James H. Bradley, Jno. G. Hurkamp, Geo. W. Wroten,
   Common Councilmen.

The Mayor stated that the Council had been convened pursuant to adjournment to receive the report of the Special Committee appointed at the last meeting of the Council in regard to clearing the wrecks out of the river.

The Committee made a verbal report through Mr. E.M. Braxton after which, on Motion, Capt. Dawes was heard upon the matter under consideration.

On motion, Mr. Richardson was also heard.

On motion, Resolved that be requested to proceed to Baltimore, and make application in the name of this body, to merchants trading with Fredericksburg, and such others as may be disposed to contribute, to subscriptions to aid in making our harbour navigable, And that a list be kept of those subscribing, which shall be published in one or more of our town papers.

Ordered, that the blank in the foregoing resolution be filled with the name of Mr. E.M. Braxton, his expenses to be paid by the Corporation.

Ordered, that a Commission of ten per cent be allowed Mr. E.M. Braxton, upon the amount subscribed through his exertions in Baltimore.

A bill of J.L. Marye, Jr. amounting to $6.50 for his expenses in visiting Richmond by request of the Council was ordered to be paid.

On motion, Resolved that the Council accept the proposition of Mr. Saml. Richardson in regard to removing the five wrecks now obstructing the navigation of the Rappahannock River, provided the necessary funds can be raised.

Mr. Bradley moved that the order of the Council passed on the 24th October 1866 in regard to the weighing of Coal be rescinded, which being seconded, was put to the vote and the motion was lost.

And then the Council adjourned.

[M. Slaughter, Mayor]

At a regular meeting of the Common Council of the Town of Fredericksburg held at the Council Chamber on Tuesday the 26th day of March 1867.

Present– M. Slaughter, Mayor
Wm. H. Cunningham, A.P. Rowe, Jos. W. Sener, Jas. McGuire, Jas. H. Bradley, J.G. Hurkamp, J.J. Young,
        Common Councilmen.

In obedience to the order of the Council passed on the 24th day of October 1866, the Clerk of the Council reported the following ordinance

"Be it ordained by the Mayor and Commonalty of the Town of Fredericksburg, that if the owner or consignee of any anthracite Coal brought to this town, shall sell the same and have it delivered without having such coal weighed at the Corporation Scales, allowing 2240 pounds to the ton, said owner or consignee shall forfeit and pay   for every ton of such coal so sold and delivered."

On Motion made and duly Seconded, the ordinance was adopted.

On Motion, the blank in the ordinance was filled with the amount of one dollar, so as to read "shall forfeit and pay one dollar for every ton of Coal so sold and delivered."

On motion of Mr. James McGuire, Resolved that the Public Property Committee be instructed, before renting the Hay Scales, to reserve to the Corporation the right to weigh all anthracite Coal sold and delivered in the said Corporation.

And then the Council adjourned.

[M. Slaughter, Mayor]

At a Called Meeting of the Common Council of the Town of Fredericksburg held at the Council Chamber on Friday evening March 29th 1867.

Present– M. Slaughter, Mayor
Thos. F. Knox, Recorder
Wm. H. Cunningham, Jos. W. Sener, Jas. W. Ford, E.M. Braxton, Geo. W. Wroten, J.G. Hurkamp, Wm. A. Little, A.P. Rowe, Jas. McGuire, Jas. H. Bradley,
Common Councilmen.

The Mayor stated that the Council had been convened at the request of members to take into consideration the ordinance now in force in regard to the weighing of Anthracite Coal.

The Mayor then read a communication from sundry coal dealers requesting a repeal of the ordinance regarding all anthracite Coal to be weighed at the Corporation Scales–Whereupon Mr. Knox, moved the following:

Be it ordained by the Mayor and Commonalty of the Town of Fredericksburg, that the ordinance passed on the 26th day of March 1867, requiring "all anthracite coal to be weighed at the Corporation Scales," be and it is hereby repealed – which being seconded, was put to the vote, the yeas & nays being called for

Ayes– Messrs. Knox & Bradley………………………..2
Noes– Messrs. Cunningham, Sener, Ford, Braxton, Wroten, Hurkamp,
Little, Rowe & McGuire………………..9
And so Mr. Knox"s Motion was lost.

Mr. Bradley moved that the present Coal Measurer be dismissed, which was seconded.

By permission, Messrs. R.W. Adams and James Hayes, were heard, when the vote was taken on Mr. Bradley's motion, and this [the] motion was lost.

And then the Council adjourned.

[M. Slaughter, Mayor]

At a called meeting of the Common Council of the Town of Fredericksburg held at the Council Chamber on Wednesday April 10th, 1867.

Present– M. Slaughter, Mayor

Thos. F. Knox, Recorder

E.M. Braxton, A.P. Rowe, J.W. Ford, J.J. Young, Wm. A. Little, Jos. W. Sener, James McGuire,

Common Councilmen.

The Mayor stated that the Council had been convened for the purpose of receiving the report of Major E.M. Braxton, of his mission to Baltimore.

Maj. Braxton then made a verbal report, which, on Motion was received and adopted and the Committee discharged.

The Mayor then read a Communication from E.T. Haynie, asking leave to retain the booth which he has erected at the Corner of Main & Commerce Streets, And on motion, permission was granted him to do so at the pleasure of the Council, on which Motion the Ayes & Noes were called for and Mr. Braxton was excused from voting.[28]

Ayes– Messrs. Knox, Rowe, Young, Little & McGuire..................5

Noes– " Sener & Ford...2

So the permission was granted.

The Subject of clearing the five wrecks obstructing the navigation of the Rappahannock River, was then taken up and Mr. Richardson, by consent, was heard.

Ordered, that the night police be dispensed with on the first of May next.

The following resolution offered by Mr. Little was adopted [viz]:

Resolved that our Delegate in the Legislature be requested to obtain the necessary legislation to authorize this Corporation to issue its bonds payable from two to ten years to the amount of $3250—to be expended in paying for removal of the obstructions in the River and Harbor of Fredericksburg, and that the Corporation be authorized to impose a tax on the Wharf owners at Fredericksburg in order to assist in defraying the expenses of removing said obstructions from the Harbor.

2nd That the Mayor be requested to communicate these resolutions to our Delegate.

And then the Council adjourned.

At a Called Meeting of the Common Council of the Town of Fredericksburg held at the Council Chamber on Monday May 13th, 1867.

Present– M. Slaughter, Mayor

Thos. F. Knox, Recorder

Wm. A. Little, Jos. W. Sener, Jas. H. Bradley, Jas. McGuire, J.G. Hurkamp, Jas. W. Ford, J.J. Young,

Common Councilmen.

The Mayor stated that the Council had been convened at the instance of some of the members.

On Motion, Mr. C.W. Wallace was heard on the part of Mr. Richardson in regard to clearing the wrecks out of the river. Mr. Richardson himself was also by consent heard.

On Motion of Mr. Young, Resolved that the Mayor be requested and instructed to employ Counsel to attend to the interests of the Corporation in the matter of the contract with Saml. P. Richardson for removing the obstructions in the Channel of the River, Said contract to be on the terms of the proposal submitted by Mr. Richardson to the Council and the $3250 - of Corporation bonds to be issued at ten years and in instalments as the work progresses. And when the work is properly done and so reported on by some party competent to do so, then the balance of said bonds to be issued.

The Mayor then read a communication from sundry Citizens in regard to digging a well at or near the corner of Frederick & Charlotte [Charles] Streets, which on Motion was referred to the Pump Committee, with instructions to take such action as in their judgment may seem necessary.

The Mayor read a Communication from Joseph E. Lowley and also one from Dr. Wm. S. Scott, which on Motion were laid on the table.

The Mayor also read a Communication from J.H. Myer in regard to the booth at the corner of Main & William Streets, and by consent [Mr.] W.C. Wallace was heard, when on Motion the Communication was laid on the table.

On Motion, ordered that Edwd. T. Haynie be summoned to appear before the Council at its next meeting to show cause why the permission heretofore granted him for keeping a booth at the corner of Main & Commerce Streets should not be withdrawn.

On Motion, Mr. Hurkamp was excused.

The Mayor presented a communication from sundry Citizens in regard to the Chimney on the old Shakepeare lot, which on Motion was referred to the Street Committee and the Superintendent of Streets, with instructions to report to the next meeting of the Council.

The Mayor then read a communication from the Board of Health in regard to the Condition of the town, which [was] on Motion, was received and laid on the table.

And then the Council adjourned.

[M. Slaughter, Mayor]

At a regular meeting of the Common Council of the Town of Fredericksburg, held at the Council Chamber on Tuesday evening May 28th, 1867.

Present– M. Slaughter, Mayor
Wm. A. Little, James McGuire, J.G. Hurkamp, E.M. Braxton, J.W. Sener, Jas. W. Ford, Wm. H. Cunningham,
Common Councilmen.

The Mayor presented a Communication from Col. C.M. Braxton, Surveyor of the Corporation, enclosing the Map of the town ordered some time ago.

On Motion, ordered that the bills of Col. Braxton for preparing the above mentioned map amounting to One Hundred dollars be paid.

On Motion, the Superintendent of Streets is directed to remove the Corporation Stones, specified in the communication of Col. Braxton and to have them placed in their proper positions under the supervision of the [Town] Surveyor.

On Motion, ordered that a Committee of three of which the Mayor shall be Chairman, be appointed to examine into the accuracy of the Map prepared by the Town Surveyor, to report to the next meeting of the Council.

The following were appointed the Committee, Messrs. Slaughter, Mayor, Little and R.W. Hart.

On Motion, ordered that the Public Property Committee have the said map varnished and neatly framed.

The Street Committee, to whom was referred the Communication of sundry Citizens in regard to the Chimney on the old Shakespeare lot, having reported to the Council that they consider the said Chimney and wall to be in a dangerous condition and that it should be taken down. Ordered that the owners of the said property have the said Chimney and Wall taken down within ten days from this date, and in the event of their failure to do so, in the time specified, the Superintendent of Streets is directed to have the same taken down, the expense to be recovered by warrant from the owners.

The Mayor presented a petition from Sundry Citizens of the town praying for a bridge to be placed over Marye's Canal on Charlotte Street, which on Motion was referred to the Street Committee with instructions to have a bridge built, if in their judgment it is expedient.[29]

Mr. Jos. W. Sener, by note in writing addressed to the Council, tendered his resignation as a member of the Council, which [was] on Motion was laid on the table.

Mr. Wm. A. Little, who was employed by the Mayor under the instructions of the Council, to prepare a Contract with Mr. Saml. Richardson for removing the five wrecks now obstructing the Channel of the River, presented and read the Contract which he had prepared, and which was already signed by Mr. Richardson, and on motion the Mayor was instructed to sign the same on the part of the Corporation.

A bill of Mr. Wm. A. Little for preparing and adjusting the above contract amounting to twenty five dollars is ordered to be paid.

Ordered that a meeting of the Common Council shall be held on Friday evening next at 8 o'clock.

And then the Council adjourned.

[M. Slaughter, Mayor]

At an adjourned meeting of the Common Council held at the Council Chamber on Friday evening May 31st, 1867.

Present– M. Slaughter, Mayor
Thos. F. Knox, Recorder

Wm. A. Little, E.M. Braxton, Jas. W. Ford, Jas. McGuire, J.G. Hurkamp, J.H. Bradley, A.P. Rowe, J.W. Sener, Wm. H. Cunningham, J.J. Young,
Common Councilmen.

The Mayor stated that the Council had met pursuant to adjournment Tuesday evening.

On Motion, Capt. R.D. Minor, was heard on the subject of removing the wrecks now obstructing the Channel of the river.

E.T. Haynie appeared before the Council in obedience to the rule served upon him, by order of the Council at a previous meeting and was represented by his Counsel, Mr. E.M. Braxton, who presented a petition from sundry citizens, property holders and tenants in the neighborhood asking that Mr. Haynie be allowed to continue or retain the booth erected by him at the Corner of Main and Commerce Streets.

On motion, Mr. James B. Sener was heard and presented a petition asking that the said booth should be removed.

Mr. J.J. Young moved that Mr. Haynie be allowed to retain his booth in its present position, which being seconded, the Yeas and Nays were called for and resulted as follows:

Yeas– Messrs. Little, McGuire, Knox and Young..........................4
Nays– Messrs. Ford, Hurkamp, Bradley, Rowe, Sener and
Cunningham...6

and so the motion was lost.

Mr. Thos. F. Knox Moved that the privilege heretofore allowed Mr. E.T. Haynie to retain his booth be withdrawn to take effect on the 1st day of October 1867, which Mr. Rowe moved to amend by withdrawing the leave, to take effect at the end of Sixty days, and the question coming up on the amendment and a division called for, Mr. Rowe's amendment was adopted.

On Motion, ordered that Mr. Haynie be required to remove his both in the next Sixty days.

A bill of John B. Larkin amounting to $1 50/100 was ordered to be paid.

On Motion, ordered that the tax of $2 00/100 paid by Rev. J.W. Gilmer for 1865 be refunded to him, as he was not a resident at the time.

And then the Council adjourned.

[M. Slaughter, Mayor]

At a Called Meeting of the Common Council of the Town of Fredericksburg held at the Council Chamber on Friday evening June 7th, 1867.

Present– E.M. Braxton and J.H. Bradley
              Common Councilmen.

There being no quorum present, the Council stood adjourned.

At a regular meeting of the Common Council of the Town of Fredericksburg held at the Council Chamber on Tuesday the 25th day of June 1867.

Present– M. Slaughter, Mayor
Wm. A. Little, Jas. H. Bradley, Wm. H. Cunningham, James McGuire, E.M. Braxton, Jos. W. Sener, J.G. Hurkamp, G.W. Wroten,
        Common Councilmen.

The Finance Committee presented a report recommending a tax bill for the current year, which on Motion, Made and Seconded, was adopted, and the Chamberlain is directed to prepare an Ordinance in accordance therewith.

By unanimous consent, the proposition of Mr. Jos.E. Lowley, which was laid on the table at a previous meeting, is permitted to be withdrawn.

On Motion of Mr. E.M. Braxton, Made and Seconded, Resolved that the owners and lessees of wharves [property] within the Corporation of Fredericksburg, have permission to erect Scales on their respective wharves by which the Weigher and Measurer of Coal is hereby authorized to weigh the Coal now required to be weighed at the Corporation Hay Scales.

On motion of Mr. J.W. Sener—

Resolved, that the Chamberlain be requested to furnish [this Council] a Statement of all moneys paid by him for repairs, or for new pumps from the first of April last to this date, including bills for same.

On Motion, the use of the upper room in the Town Hall is granted to John F. Scott and George Aler, officers of the "Friends of Temperance Society," for the use of their Society during the pleasure of the Council.

On motion of Mr. J.W. Sener -

Resolved, that the Street Committee, with the assistance of the Town Surveyor, be and they are hereby instructed to ascertain accurately how much of Sophia Street has been taken up by buildings, fencing or otherwise, and report what action is necessary to protect the Corporation from further injury, and also whether it will be to the interest of the Corporation to condemn and sell a part of Said Street.[30]

On motion of Mr. Wm. A. Little –

Resolved that the Public Property Committee be and they are hereby instructed to investigate and report to the Council the situation of the Mercer Square property, and what privileges, if any, have been granted to any parties in regard to the said property, and at what price said property can be sold, payable in the bonds of the Corporation.

It being reported that [a] blacksmith shop has been put up at the foot of Charles Street, which is said to be in the said Street, Ordered that the Street Committee be instructed to enquire into the facts of the case and to report to the next meeting of the Council.[31]

And then the Council adjourned.

[M. Slaughter, Mayor]

At a Called Meeting of the Common Council of the Town of Fredericksburg held at the Council Chamber on Tuesday the 9th day of July 1867.

Present– M. Slaughter, Mayor
Thos. F. Knox, Recorder
A.P. Rowe, J.H. Bradley, E.M. Braxton, Jas. McGuire, John J. Young, Wm. H. Cunningham, J.G. Hurkamp,
Common Councilmen.

The Mayor stated that the Council had been called to receive a report from the Committee appointed in the Contract entered into with Mr. Saml. Richardson, which report was [then] read, from which it appears that Mr. Richardson has complied with first part of the Contract, and on Motion, Ordered that the first installment of the bonds called for by the [said] contract, amounting to the sum of One thousand dollars, viz: two bonds of five hundred dollars each, bearing date on the day of delivery and payable respectively two and three years after date, with interest at six per cent per Annum, be executed by the Mayor and Chamberlain, and delivered to Mr. Richardson.

Mr. Rowe presented a proposition from Mr. C.S. Scott, proposing to enclose the Burying Ground on Prince Edward Street, he to have the privilege of using the same for a period to be fixed upon hereafter, And on Motion, Mr. Scott was heard on the Matter, When Mr. Hurkamp moved that the whole subject be referred to the Public Property Committee to examine into the subject and also to inquire into the cost of repairing the Wall around the said Burying Ground. Mr. Bradley offered [as] an amendment to Mr. Hurkamp's motion, that the Public Property Committee be instructed to have the said Burying Ground enclosed in as economical a manner as possible. Mr. McGuire moved to lay the whole matter on the table, which motion was lost, and the question recurring on the amendment of Mr. Bradley, it was adopted.[32]

On Motion, Ordered that Mr. C.S. Scott be permitted to build a toll house at this end of his bridge on each side of Commerce Street the same to be held by him at the discretion of the Council.

And then the Council adjourned.

[M. Slaughter, Mayor]

At a regular meeting of the Common Council of the Town of Fredericksburg, held at the Council Chamber on Tuesday July 23rd, 1867.
Present– M. Slaughter, Mayor
Thos. F. Knox, Recorder
James McGuire, A.P. Rowe, Jno. J. Young, J.G. Hurkamp, E.M. Braxton, Geo. W. Wroten, Jas. H. Bradley and J.W. Ford, Common Councilmen.

The Public Property Committee, through its Chairman [Mr. McGuire], made a verbal report in regard to the "Mercer Square" property, now in the possession of the Fredericksburg Agricultural Society, unanimously recommending that the Corporation should resume the control of the said property, but that they had not been able to ascertain at what price the said property could be sold payable in the bonds of the Corporation.

On Motion, Maj. J.H. Kelley, Secy. of the Agricultural Society was heard on the report of the Pub. Prop. Com., when Mr. Bradley moved that the resolution passed on the 15th of February 1866 granting permission of [to] the Fredg. Agricultural Society to resume possession of the Mercer Square property upon the terms and conditions of its former occupation before the War, be revoked, which motion being seconded, was passed by a vote of six to three.

The Mayor read a communication from a large number of Citizens of the Town asking that the previous action of the Council requiring E.T. Haynie to remove his booth at the corner of Main & Commerce Street be revoked and that Mr. Haynie be allowed to remain undisturbed for the present. When Mr. Knox moved that the action [of the Council] of May 31st requiring E.T. Haynie to remove his booth in sixty days, be rescinded, which was adopted - Mr. E.M. Braxton declining to vote.

Mr. Knox then moved that Mr. E.T. Haynie be allowed to retain his booth at the Corner of Main & Commerce St. until the 1st day of May 1868, which being seconded was adopted. Mr. E.M. Braxton declining to vote.

On Motion, Resolved that the Rappahannock Agricultural Society be allowed to hold their annual fairs on the Mercer Square property until the said property is disposed of.[33]

An Ordinance imposing taxes for the year 1867 was passed and is in [the] words & figures following to wit:

1st Be it Ordained by the Mayor & Common Council of the Town of Fredericksburg, that their [there] shall be levied & collected on persons, property & other subjects of the Town of Fred[erick]sburg. to defray the expenses of the Corporation for the year ending on the 3rd Monday in March 1868 the taxes following to Wit

2nd On Real Estate fifty cents in every hundred dollars value thereof, agreeable to the Commissioners books.

3rd On personal property fifty cents in every hundred dollars value thereof, agreeable to the Commissioners books.

4 On each white or cold. male above the age of twenty one years two (2) dollars.

5th On all licenses and other subjects, assessed with State taxes within the Corporation of Fredericksburg (except brokers who are taxed ¼ of State tax) 50 per Cent of the State tax for the year 1867 assessed thereon, and excepting theatrical & other exhibitions, which are taxed under an Ordinance of the Corporation.

6th And it is further ordered that One half of the tax so assessed by this bill be received in the interest past due on the bonds of the Corporation of Fredsbg. at par.

A bill of Dr. Wm. S. Scott for attending a Coroner inquest amounting to five Dollars is ordered to be paid.

A bill of M. Slaughter for acting as Coroner & holding an inquest amounting to five dollars is ordered to be paid.

On motion, Ordered that the salary of the Superintendent of Streets be paid [fixed] at the rate of Two Hundred dollars per Annum from this date.

And then the Council adjourned.

[M. Slaughter, Mayor]

This 1867 map was developed by Carter M. Braxton. Note the fairgrounds/Mercer Square area where the Federal's attacked in December 1862. The Telegraph Road/Sunken Road is not shown as it was then beyond the municipal boundary.

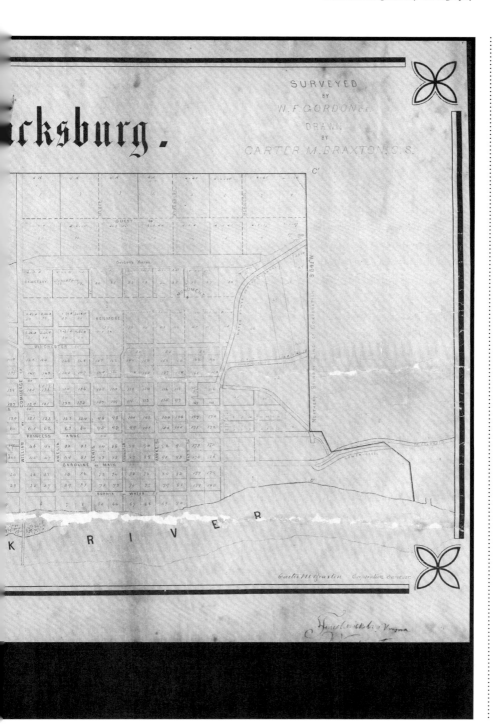

At a Stated [Called] meeting of the Common Council held at the Council Chamber Wednesday July 24th, 1867.

Present– M. Slaughter, Mayor
　　　　　Thos. F. Knox, Recorder
E.M. Braxton, G.W. Wroten, J.G. Hurkamp, Jas. McGuire, Jas. H. Bradley, Jas. W. Ford, Wm. H. Cunningham, A.P. Rowe.

The Mayor stated that the Council had been called to receive a report from the Committee appointed to superintend the removal of the Wrecks from the River which report was then read by the Mayor.

On motion, Ordered that the second instalment of the bonds called for by the contract of the Corporation with Mr. Saml. Richardson amounting to the sum of One Thousand dollars in [viz], two bonds for the sum of five hundred dollars each, bearing date on the day of delivery and payable respectively four & six years after date, with interest at six per Centum per Annum, be executed by the Mayor & Chamberlain and delivered to Mr. Richardson.

On motion, ordered that the [this] Council adjourn till Saturday evening July 27th [1867] at 7 ½ O'clock.

　　　　　　　　　　　　　　　　[M. Slaughter, Mayor]

At a called meeting of the Common Council of the Town of Fredericksburg held on Monday Augt. 12, 1867.

Present– M. Slaughter, Mayor
　　　　　Geo. W. Wroten, E.M. Braxton.

There being no quorum present the Council stood adjourned.

At a called meeting of the Common Council of the Town of Fredericksburg held on Tuesday Augt. 13, 1867.

Present– M. Slaughter, Mayor
　　　　　E.M. Braxton, Jas. McGuire.

There being no quorum present, the Council stood adjourned.

At a called meeting of the Common Council of the Town of Fredericksburg held on Wednesday Augt. 14th 1867.

Present– M. Slaughter, Mayor
E.M. Braxton, Jas. McGuire, Jas. H. Bradley.

There being no quorum present the Council stood adjnd.

At a called meeting of the [Common Council of the] Town of Fredericksburg held on Thursday Augt. 15th, 1867.

Present– M. Slaughter, Mayor
E.M. Braxton, J.G. Hurkamp, Jno. J. Young, Jas. W. Ford, Jas. H. Bradley, Wm. H. Cunningham, Jas. McGuire, Thos. F. Knox, Wm. A. Little.

The Mayor stated that the Council had been called to receive a report from the Committee appointed to superintend the removal of the wrecks from the River, which report was then read and received and ordered to be filed, And it appearing that Mr. Saml. Richardson has completed his contract for removing five wrecks from the Channel of the River, on motion of Mr. Bradley, Ordered that the third and last installment of the bonds called for by the said Contract amounting to the sum of Twelve hundred & fifty dollars, Viz: Two bonds for the sum of five hundred dollars each, and one bond for the sum of two hundred & fifty dollars, payable respectively, Eight, Nine & Ten Years after date and bearing interest at six per Centum per Annum, be executed by the Mayor & Chamberlain and delivered to Mr. Saml. Richardson being in full for the amount due him under the said Contract.

And then the Council adjourned.

[M. Slaughter, Mayor]

At a Regular meeting of the Common Council of held at the Council Chamber, August 27th 1867.

Present– M. Slaughter, Mayor
A.P. Rowe, Geo. W. Wroten, Jas. McGuire, J.H. Bradley, Jas. W. Ford, Jno. J. Young and Wm. H. Cunningham.

The Mayor presented a communication from the 2nd Lieut. Hector Sears, Military Commissioner enclosing an order from the H[ea]d. Quarters First Military District State of V[irgini]a. in regard to the care of all indigent persons in the [this] Corporation without respect to Color & also a Communication from the President of the Board of Overseers of the Poor upon the same subject, which communication & order were then read.[34]

On motion of Jas. H. Bradley the following response to the communication of Lieut. Sears, enclosing General Order No. 51, H[ea]d. Quarters first Military District State of Virginia and also a communication from President Board of Overseer of Poor was adopted and ordered to be spread upon the minutes of the Council.

"In reply to the communication submitted to the Common Council of Fredericksburg Lieut. Hector Sears, enclosing communication from the President of the Board of Overseers of the Poor, in regard to providing means for support of paupers &c., this Council begs leave respectfully to state that they have always endeavoured (sic) & even in the most disastrous period of their history, during & since the War, succeeded in providing means for the support of such paupers, white & [or] black, as may have been properly chargeable to the Corporation, by means of permanent residence lawfully acquired in the Town. The question of color has never arisen in the Board of Overseers, when the necessity for relief was apparent. Free Negroes & Whites shared alike, before and during the War, when the poor fund was distributed, and the Emancipation of the Negro[es] in our midst has made no difference in this regard, except to diminish the subject[s] of taxation & the resources of the Town, while it has greatly increased the number[s] properly chargeable for support upon the Community. The situation of this community, its poverty and its financial condition is truly set forth in the enclosed communication from the President of the Overseers of the Poor, which this Council beg leave to adopt & endorse, It is further proper and this Council herein respectfully state[s] that by the operation[s] of the Freedsman [Freedmen's] Bureau in Fred[erick]sb[ur]g. and that without consultation with or any authority from the Municipal Authorities of the [this] Town, there have been collected from the adjoining Counties a number of blind, lame, sick and pauper Negroes, who have subsisted upon supplies from [furnished by] said Bureau, and whom this Council has reason to fear it is proposed to turn over to us to support, & they beg leave respectfully to represent to Lieut. Sears & through him to Genl. Schofield the manifest & palpable injustice of this course, that it is contrary to our municipal and to our State legislation and if required will be forced upon an already overburdened & impoverished community, without color of law, by the strong arm of Military [power & law]. We do not believe that the Military authorities in Va. can lend themselves to any such invasion of the legal rights of this community & their past record assures us of their future action, and we respectfully ask that all paupers who may have been thus collected and maintained here by the Freedsman's Bureau may be returned to the City or County of their former residence, where they are by law properly chargeable, and this Corporation & Council will to the utmost of its means & resources endeavor to supply the necessities of those who are lawfully & properly chargeable upon the Corporation of Fredericksburg. Having thus respectfully submitted our views in the premises, we return the Communication named and ask that this appeal to Genl. Schofield may accompany them to HeadQuarters." [35]

On motion, ordered that the Clerk of the Council prepare a certified copy of the foregoing appeal & enclose the same to Lieut. Hector Sears, Military Commissioner &c. with the request that he will forward the same, together with the Communication of the President of the Board of Overseers of the Poor, to Maj. Genl. S.M. Schofield for his action.

And then the Council adjourned.

[M. Slaughter, Mayor]

At a called meeting of the Common Council held at the Council Chamber on Wednesday Sept. 4th, 1867.

Present– M. Slaughter, Mayor

Geo. W. Wroten, E.M. Braxton, Jas. McGuire, A.P. Rowe.

There being no quorum present the Council stood adjourned.

At a Called Meeting of the Common Council held at the Council Chamber on Monday Sept. 9th, 1867.

Present– M. Slaughter, Mayor

       Thos. F. Knox, Recorder

A.P. Rowe, Geo. W. Wroten, J.G. Hurkamp, Jas. H. Bradley, Jas. McGuire.

There being no quorum present, the Council stood adjourned.

At a Regular Meeting of the Common Council of the Town of Fredsburg held at the Council Chamber on Tuesday the 24th day of September 1867.

Present– M. Slaughter, Mayor

    Thos. F. Knox, Recorder

Geo. W. Wroten, Jno. J. Young, Wm. H. Cunningham, E.M. Braxton, Jas. McGuire, Jas. H. Bradley, J.G. Hurkamp.

The Mayor presented & read a communication from Mr. Jas. Hayes enclosing a communication from Lieut. Hector Sears, in regard to the colored paupers now in the Hospital for Freedmen in this Town–And on motion of Mr. Jas. H. Bradley, this Council expresses its readiness & willingness to take charge & care for all colored paupers who were residents of the Town on the 1st day of January 1861 & the Mayor is requested to communicate the sense of the Council to the President of the Board of Overseers of the Poor.[36]

The Mayor presented his report in writing in regard to the manner in which the Police Officers have discharged their duties during the last three months—Which report on motion of Mr. Geo. W. Wroten was received and the Chamberlain was instructed to pay the Quarter salary now due to J.S.G. Timberlake one of the Police Officers.

On motion of Mr. Geo. W. Wroten, Ordered that Jas. A. Taylor be dismissed from office as a Police Officer of this Corporation.

Mr. Bradley moved that the Council proceed at once to the election of three night Policemen—Which motion Mr. McGuire moved to amend by substituting two in place of three, which amendment not being seconded was withdrawn—and the question being taken on Mr. Bradley's motion it was resolved that three night Policemen be elected to serve during the pleasure of the Council.

On motion of Mr. Bradley ordered that the compensation of the night Police be fixed at One hundred & fifty cents per day—and to be paid as heretofore.

The Mayor then read to the Council the application of sundry Citizens for the Office of night Policemen & the ballot being circulated the following named persons were elected as night Policemen, Viz: Geo. H. Timberlake, Martin Cahill and Jno. B. Larkin.

The Mayor presented a Communication from Mr. A.S. McKenney which on motion was referred to the Pub. Prop. Committee, with the [a] request that they report on the same at the next meeting of the Council.

Mr. Braxton moved that the Ordinance passed on the 26th day of Mar. 1867 as an amendment to the old Ordinance in regard to the weighing of Anthracite Coal be repealed–which Mr. McMGuire moved to amend as follows, "that the Ordinance now in force in regard to the weighing of Coal remain in force, provided that nothing in this Ordinance shall be construed to apply to Coal which may be sold & delivered from the Coalyards," and the question being taken on the amendment of Mr. McGuire it was adopted.

The Mayor presented a communication from Lt. Col. Johnson desiring to procure the room in the south end of the Court House for the use of a free Colored School and on motion of Mr. Braxton the Chairman of the Pub[lic] Prop[erty] Committee be instructed to inform Col. Johnson that the Council respectfully decline to rent the room for that purpose.[37]

Geo. H. Timberlake and Jno. B. Larkin, Night Policemen appeared and took the Oath[s] of Office before M. Slaughter, Esq., Mayor.

And then the Council adjourned.

[M. Slaughter, Mayor]

At a called meeting of the Common Council of the Town of Fredericksburg, held at the Council Chamber on Friday the 25th day of October 1867.

Present– Wm. A. Little, Jas. H. Bradley, Jas. W. Ford & A.P. Rowe.

There being no quorum present, the Council stood adjourned.

At a Called Meeting of the Common Council of the Town of Fredericksburg held on Saturday October 26th, 1867.

Present– M. Slaughter, Mayor
Geo. W. Wroten, Jas. H. Bradley, Wm. H. Cunningham.

There being no quorum present, the Council stood adjourned.

At a regular meeting of the Common Council of the Town of Fredericksburg held on Tuesday Nov. 26, 1867.

Present– M. Slaughter, Mayor
E.M. Braxton, Wm. A. Little, Geo. W. Wroten, Jas. McGuire, Jno. G. Hurkamp, Ab. P. Rowe, Wm. H. Cunningham & Jas H. Bradley.

The Mayor presented a communication from W.H. Revere in regard to the assessment of his property in the Town of Fredg. which on motion made & seconded, was referred to the Commissioner of the Revenue for his action.

On motion of Mr. E.M. Braxton, Ordered that the Quarter's salary due on the 18th day of September 1867 to Jas. A. Taylor for his services as Police Officer, be paid to him by the Chamberlain.

(On motion of Mr. J.G. Hurkamp) St. Geo. R. Fitzhugh, Esq., by permission of the Council presented a communication from Mr. J.B. Ficklen in regard to Ground Rent due by him to the Corporation, which (x) was referred to the finance Committee for settlement.

Mr. Fitzhugh also presented a proposition from Mr. Ficklen to purchase the interest of the Corporation in the property now held by him upon a lien for lives, which on motion made and seconded was referred to the Pub[lic] Prop[erty] Committee, with instructions to report to the next meeting of the Council & especially to report the value of the Corporation's interest in the said property.

Mr. Bradley moved that two additional night watches [watchmen] be appointed to serve during the pleasure of the Council, which being duly seconded, the Ayes & Nays [Noes] were called for, the vote resulted as follows:

Ayes– Messrs. Braxton, Little, Wroten, Rowe, Cunningham & Bradley
Noes– Messrs. McGuire & Hurkamp

and the motion was adopted.

The Mayor then read to the Council the application of sundry persons for appointment as Night Watchmen, & Mr. Jas. A. Taylor & Wm. H. Deshazo were also put in nomination and the ballot being had resulted in the election of T.W. Roberts and Chas. W. Edrington, who being present were sworn into office by the Mayor.

And then the Council adjourned.

[M. Slaughter, Mayor]

❦ NOTES ❧

1. Reconstruction has been misrepresented and misunderstood, but better use of source material has led to stronger analysis and more balanced interpretations. Eric Foner has been a leading scholar of the reconstruction era and his writing has been a significant corrective in this still-controversial field. James McPherson's excellent work has also informed this very brief summary. Eric Foner, *Reconstruction: America's Unfinished Revolution, 1863-1877* (New York: Harper & Row, 1988); James M. McPherson, *Abraham Lincoln and the Second American Revolution* (New York: Oxford University Press, 1990).
2. The Farmer's Hotel was located on the southwest corner of Hanover and Caroline Streets.
3. Following the war, thousands of bodies were recovered from various parts of the town and reinterred in cemeteries. Wrecked buildings were everywhere, harboring rodents and other potential sources of disease. Drainage facilities also needed immediate attention.
4. A suspension of the rules allows a legislative body to take action on an item where the typical procedure would be to wait until the next meeting.
5. The marsh and canal referenced here were part of the Fredericksburg battlefield, often referred to as the "canal ditch" in wartime accounts and National Park Service interpretive materials.
6. Mercer Square was located on the open area in front of the Confederate position at Marye's Heights.
7. Ailanthus altissima is a deciduous tree of Chinese origins. It was brought the America in the eighteenth century and became popular as a street tree in the nineteenth century. It soon became recognized as an unwelcome invasive and the current Fredericksburg City Code still prohibits its use as a street tree.
8. A telegraph line had already been established through Fredericksburg before the Civil War. The current Lafayette Boulevard (U.S. Route 1 Business) had been called Telegraph Road. C.C. Wellford had offices at the southwest corner of Caroline and George Streets (824 and 826 Caroline Street). Mr. Carter's house was a few doors away, at 820 Caroline Street.
9. The Freedmen's Court had been set up by the Bureau of Refugees, Freedmen and Abandoned Lands (commonly called the Freedmen's Bureau) to adjudicate disputes involving African Americans. A com-

mission typically included three members—a person from the Bureau, a freedman, and a local representative. Southerners viewed the Freedmen's Bureau as an unwelcome intrusion into their local affairs and were not very supportive.

10. In this instance, the local government was bringing its statutes into line with the legal abolition of slavery, which had recently occurred through ratification of the Thirteenth Amendment to the U.S. Constitution.
11. John L. Marye was the owner of the Kenmore Company, which maintained the canal as a raceway.
12. The Kenmore drainage ditch has always collected a large part of Fredericksburg's runoff and has been modified and improved to be as efficient as possible. Still, an exceptionally strong rainstorm will cause some degree of flooding.
13. The basin refers to the canal turning basin, which constituted the downstream terminus of the Rappahannock Navigation System. The canal's navigation function had become limited, but as a power canal it supported several large mills.
14. The 1866 election was conducted as local elections had always been. A few weeks later, however, President Andrew Johnson would declare the rebellion over, without addressing ongoing problems with Southern state governments refusing to recognize the new status of freed slaves and former free blacks as citizens. The political conflict between Johnson and Congress, which was more committed to addressing lingering issues related to the war, would eventually result in the Federal government starting over with reconstruction, under martial law.
15. One can appreciate that the upper class citizens of Fredericksburg took on the obligations of citizenship and local leadership, but there was also the benefit of a salary in hard times, made possible by a range of taxes on businesses and working people.
16. Frederick Theodore Miller has been the subject of two articles in this journal (2004, 2005). A daguerian was someone who could produce daguerreotypes, a type of early photography.
17. Dr. Wellford's house was at today's 802-804 Princess Anne Street.
18. Taxes levied in Southern towns routinely shifted much of the burden away from landowners and on to working folks. The levy of real estate taxes appears fair, but was based on property assessments, which could be manipulated. Personal property taxes, on the other hand, were more

rigidly applied and routinely fell on persons who needed tools and equipment to make a living. The tax on "colored males" is clearly unfair.
19. The need to clear wrecked buildings and neglected lots remained an ongoing concern.
20. A fine for discharging a firearm within the corporate limits is a welcome sign of normalcy, in a place where thousands of soldiers had once engaged in furious combat.
21. Construction of the Fredericksburg & Gordonsville Railroad had begun before the Civil War, to provide a connection between the established Richmond, Fredericksburg & Potomac Railroad and the agricultural areas to the west. No tracks had been laid when the war came and this unfinished railway proved useful for moving troops rapidly across otherwise rough terrain during several of the battles fought in the area. Completing the railway promised economic benefits in the war-torn region and the line would finally be completed in 1877.
22. Alexander Walker owned many properties in the Wolfe Street area. The wall in question may have been near his house (no longer extant), at the northeast corner of Wolfe and Princess Anne Streets.
23. The Union House stood at the northeast corner of Lewis and Caroline Streets. It is not extant.
24. The Shakespeare lot was in the 800 block of Caroline Street (east side).
25. The Military Bill refers to the Reconstruction Act of 1867, passed by Congress after overriding a presidential veto. The Act divided the South into military districts, where local governments would be supervised by Federal authorities. In effect, Congress was starting Reconstruction over. Five military districts were established. The Commonwealth of Virginia comprised the First District. The Second District included North and South Carolina; the Third District Georgia, Alabama, and Florida; the Fourth District Mississippi and Arkansas; and the Fifth District Texas and Louisiana. Tennessee did not experience military occupation. Its state government had not imposed harsh codes designed to keep former slaves under control and was thus considered suitably reconstructed.
26. Major General John A. Schofield had fought in the trans-Mississippi and western theaters during the Civil War. He had also been on a diplomatic mission to France in the immediate post-war period, to resolve the matter of French troops in Mexico supporting the Emperor

Maximilian. President Johnson appointed him to head up the First Military District.
27. This letter emphasizes that Fredericksburg had come under martial law. The initials VRC refer to the Veteran Reserve Corps, also known as the Invalid Corps, which made use of wounded and disabled soldiers who were no longer fit for field duty, but could handle other, more limited duties. The initials RF & AL abbreviates the Bureau of Refugees, Freedmen & Abandoned Lands (the Freedmen's Bureau).
28. Main and Commerce Streets are currently called Caroline and William Streets.
29. This bridge was not a replacement for a Civil War period bridge, but rather a new bridge.
30. Sophia Street runs adjacent to the Rappahannock River and is prone to flooding. Significant destruction occurred in the 900, 1000, and 1300 blocks of Sophia Street. The topography dropped off from the edge of the road, so it would have been tempting for people seeking to live and work there to use a bit more of the level ground than was rightfully theirs to occupy.
31. The foot of Charles Street would have been on the south end of town. The blacksmith shop may have been located in the 200 block, where a stone foundation survives today from an earlier industrial operation and abuts the public right-of-way.
32. The Corporation Burying Ground occupied land that had belonged to St. George's parish. Following the American Revolution and disestablishment of the Anglican Church in Virginia, the town government had appropriated the property for a public burying ground and burials occurred there from 1787 through 1853. In 1860, St. George's Episcopal Church petitioned the Town Council to investigate its claim to the property, but the Civil War interrupted that process. The wall surrounding the Corporation Burying Ground had become damaged during the war and the repairs referenced in the minutes would keep animals from gaining access and rooting around the graves. By 1875, the town council came to conclusion that the burying ground had become too neglected to remain a cemetery and directed the removal of headstones and graves to other cemeteries. They then converted the land to a public park, called Hurkamp Park, which opened in 1881. The claim to the land by St. George's Church resurfaced in 1953, when the

Fredericksburg Rescue Squad asked to lease a portion of the property for a new building. By then, public usage over several generations had established public ownership.

33. As noted above, Mercer Square was the old fairgrounds on the open plain in front of Marye's Heights/Sunken Road that had been part of the Fredericksburg battlefield. Mass graves in the vicinity had been dug up after the war and the Union remains reinterred in the nearby National Cemetery.

34. Lieutenant Hector Sears had fought at Bull Run and in the Western theater with New York regiments. He had sustained an arm wound at Port Hudson, in May 1863, and been commissioned in the Veteran Reserve Corps, to serve in the Freedmen's Bureau. The Commonwealth of Virginia comprised the First Military District under the Reconstruction Act of 1867, and Lt. Sears served in the Sixth Subdistrict, which included Fredericksburg and the counties of Spotsylvania, Stafford, and King George. He witnessed firsthand the difficulty that free blacks endured in the civil courts that were run by former Confederates.

35. Caring for persons in need requires the expenditure of resources and localities are still concerned with having to care for persons from outside the jurisdiction.

36. Again, when local resources must be used to care for persons in need, the local jurisdiction is concerned that its local resources go toward helping local folks.

37. Schools for black children did not receive support from the town council. African American churches were often used as school houses, with some support from the Freedmen's Bureau. Northern white teachers came South to provide instruction. One such missionary was a woman from Ohio named Sophia Hatch, who taught students at the Shiloh Baptist Church on Sophia Street. She taught at African American schools in Fredericksburg until 1890.

This view from the National Park's property at Salem Church is what a visitor experiences on that battlefield. The ground beyond the small protected site is covered with pavement and buildings.

This view, from outside the National Park, is more revealing of the battlefield terrain. The monument suggests the proximity of the Federal line to the defending Confederates in the vicinity of the church.

Fredericksburg's Second Battlefield: Hidden but Not Forgotten

BY ERIK F. NELSON

The Central Virginia Battlefields Trust (CVBT) recently moved its offices to a building in Fredericksburg's industrial park. To the west of this new location is a wooded ridge within the Fredericksburg and Spotsylvania National Military Park, crowned with Confederate gun pits and infantry trenches. To the north is Hazel Run and the wartime unfinished railway, beyond which is Marye's Heights/Sunken Road - also part of the National Military Park. Looking out the front door is a working farm, where a Federal assault column advanced across the open ground on May 3, 1863. The Trust is headquartered on a battlefield. Neither the Trust nor the National Park Service, however, seeks to acquire and preserve that ground. The purchase price is high and its industrial context would not be suitable for incorporation into the Battlefield Park. In the realm of battlefield preservation, that land is considered lost to development. The story that unfolded there is important though, and ought not to be lost as well.

On the morning of May 3, 1863, the Union Sixth Corps, Major General John Sedgwick commanding, stood poised to attack the fortified Confederate positions at Fredericksburg. The main armies were fighting to the west, around Chancellorsville, the distant crash of battle clearly audible to the waiting troops. Also audible was artillery and small arms fire on the far left and far right of Sedgwick's line, as the opposing forces maneuvered against one another. The Southern forces remaining in Fredericksburg were considerably fewer than had halted Federal attacks in December 1862, but the Confederate position was still a strong one and Federal success was by no means assured. Sedgwick meant for his next effort to be swift and coordinated, to overcome the killing zone in front of Marye's Heights.

The Sixth Corps commander would advance four columns at once. He planned to send assault forces in brigade strength up William and Hanover Streets. A reinforced brigade would also advance in line of battle against the stone wall at the foot of the heights, but this latter force would not march out of the town and then deploy, as had occurred in December. Instead, the component units had crossed the canal ditch earlier that morning and formed in the shelter of an embankment. When the signal for an attack came, they were positioned to rapidly cross the open ground and close in on the stone wall before being blasted apart by artillery and small arms fire.[1]

South of Hazel Run, near the Trust's new office, a fourth assault column waited as well. Brigadier General Albion P. Howe had deployed his division to attack Howison Hill and Telegraph Hill (also called Lee's Hill). Howe's troops were from Vermont, New Jersey, New York, and Maine. Awaiting them in the earthworks on the ridge overlooking the open ground were infantrymen from Mississippi and Louisiana, backed up by artillery from Georgia and South Carolina. The attacking Federals would also be within range of an enfilading fire from Confederate batteries on Willis Hill, which is the southernmost feature of Marye's Heights.

When Howe heard Union artillery on this right, in Fredericksburg, he opened up with his own artillery and launched his infantry. The 77th New York Regiment had already advanced into the open ground as skirmishers. When the main line came up to the area now occupied by the building where the CVBT has its offices, about midway between a railway and the chain of hills held by Southern forces, Confederate artillery opened up with everything they had. The 26th New Jersey, a new regiment placed in the first line due to its relatively full ranks, faltered under the severe fire. Many of the rookie infantrymen gravitated toward the shelter of a large barn, while others attached themselves to the more experienced unit following in support. The 2nd Vermont Regiment, coming up behind the 26th New Jersey, moved around them, by the right flank.[2]

While Howe's men moved toward the Confederate trenches, the attack in front of Marye's Heights also unfolded swiftly. The two Federal columns moved up their respective roadways while the line of battle raced toward the stone wall. Each force struggled to maintain its momentum under severe fire. When Howe's forces had come abreast of Marye's Heights, three of his regiments veered toward the Confederate stronghold on Willis Hill, splashed across Hazel Run, and found themselves under the shelter of a railway embankment. Behind this protective earth, the 6th Vermont and 33rd New York Regiments moved quickly to the left and then charged up a draw that took them to the top of Marye's Heights. The Vermont men surged ahead of the New Yorkers and burst on to the hilltop behind two guns of Parker's Virginia battery. The 6th Maine Regiment, which had been one of the units attacking across the open ground in front of the heights, vaulted over the stone wall, bayoneted their way through the Mississippians in Sunken Road, and gained the top of the hill just seconds before the 6th Vermont. The 33rd New York Regiment followed immediately behind the Vermont men.[3]

On the left, Howe's attack continued up Telegraph (Lee's) Hill. Finding his soldiers catching their breath in the Confederate works at the bottom of the hill, Colonel Lewis A. Grant shouted: "Up now, my brave boys and give it to them." The 2nd Vermont responded by charging up the slope, joined by stalwart members of the otherwise scattered 26th New Jersey Regiment. The 33rd New York, on Marye's Heights observed the developing action, ran back down the hill, and then advanced up Telegraph Hill in support of the Vermont and the New Jersey soldiers. The 6th Vermont remained behind, ordered to deploy across Marye's Heights as skirmishers.[4]

On top of Telegraph Hill, Captain John C. Fraser's Georgia battery had been firing furiously at the approaching Federal infantry. Union counter-battery fire had exploded one of their limber chests, but the gun crews were holding their own amidst the rounds plowing in to their hilltop. As Confederate infantry filtered back in the face of the Federal attack, the artillerymen prepared to remove their guns from harm's way. The advancing Union infantry were disappearing from view in the hilly terrain and the battery commander did not want to be flanked and have his guns captured. While helping to ready the battery to pull back, a Lieutenant Fred Habersham dismounted to help a sergeant and a private who were holding skittish horses in a ravine. A Federal artillery round exploded nearby and a fragment took off half of the young officer's head. The lieutenant was from a prominent Savannah family and the artillerymen took the time to strap his mangled body to a limber so they could take him to the rear with the guns.[5]

Battle smoke added to the hellish conditions on Telegraph Hill, obscuring anyone's ability to assess what was going on. The assaulting Federals closed in on the Confederate position and shot down the Southern gunners. The Union assault force began to capture cannons, one of them with the rammer still sticking out of the muzzle. A Federal infantrymen observed that the Confederate "artillery men was gritty." On top of the hill, smoke swirled around the spent units of both sides. The Vermont soldiers saw their Southern adversaries trying to recover from the onslaught - some rallying, but others hesitating. Whoever advanced would likely prevail and the Vermont men overcame their fatigue first and pushed on, driving the Confederate infantry from the hill.[6]

The 3rd and 4th Vermont Regiments arrived in support of the 2nd Vermont. They found the attack successful and pressed on to Howison Hill. Other units had already veered toward that promontory, guided by a farm road that led to a prominent brick mansion called Braehead. As the Federals worked their way up the ravines, the Confederate batteries in that sector also pulled out and made their way to the Telegraph Road (modern Lafayette Boulevard). The Sixth Corps had gained control of the heights and would soon regroup and press on toward Chancellorsville, just a half dozen miles beyond a place called Salem Church.[7]

The remnant of the farm road that guided the Federal attack on May 3, 1863 is still visible from the CVBT's front door. If one follows it into the Fredericksburg and Spotsylvania National Military Park, however, there does not appear to be any related interpretation of the Federal attack that day. A visitor encounters metal panels identifying the Confederate trenches by those units that held that line in 1862, before the earthworks were dug. A nearby tour stop and a path, however, guide visitors to the top of Telegraph Hill, identified as Lee's Hill, where there is an exhibit shelter with several interpretive panels. One of them describes a second battle of Fredericksburg and recounts the story of Fred Habersham. The ravine where the young lieutenant was killed, however, is not on Park land and the single panel is a minor nod toward this important action.

The inevitable question is why has an entire battle been made to seem irrelevant? The answer starts with the limited amount of land acquired and protected at Fredericksburg and the manner in which the Park's early historians interpreted it. Since the Fredericksburg and Spotsylvania National Military Park was established in 1927, its staff and non-profit partners have assembled and preserved substantial tracts of land where five battles were fought, while interpreting four of them. The Chancellorsville component of this National Park includes much of the terrain where Confederate generals Robert E. Lee and Thomas J. Jackson confronted Federal commander Joseph Hooker and his powerful Union army. The sequence of historic events is dramatic. Hooker stole a march on Lee by crossing the Rappahannock River far upstream of Fredericksburg. Jackson, the legendary Stonewall, pulled together a force to stop this advance on May 1 and then met with Lee that evening to try to find a way to turn back and perhaps destroy the Northern host. They planned for Jackson to execute an extended march that would get Confederate forces on to the Federal right flank. Late in the afternoon of May 2, Jackson attacked the unprepared Union force with stunning success, but was struck down by a volley of friendly fire later that evening. The next day's fighting, from Hazel Grove to Chancellorsville, was some of the most vicious of the war and is the very heart of the National Park at Chancellorsville. At Lee's moment of victory, as Confederate forces overran the clearing at the famous crossroads, a courier rode up with news that a Union force in Fredericksburg was on the march. The Southern commander quickly dispatched troops to reinforce the Confederate units preparing to stop the approaching column at Salem Church.

The sequence of events that brought the threatening Federal force to Salem Church is not interpreted on preserved land. That part of the Chancellorsville campaign began on April 29 with the Union Sixth Corps, Major General John Sedgwick commanding, executing a diversionary river crossing south of Fredericksburg. Several days of minor maneuvering ensued while Hooker operated to the west. On May 2, Jackson's flank attack panicked the army command and Hooker ordered Sedgwick to come to Chancellorsville. The Sixth Corps advanced into Fredericksburg that night and by the morning of May 3 had secured the town and begun to probe the Confederate line. Just before midday, those Union forces attacked where the Federal army had met disaster in December, and overran the Southern position. They then marched west, toward Chancellorsville, until they encountered Lee's forces blocking their way at Salem Church. Later that night and during May 4, the two sides took position across the hills and ravines west of Fredericksburg. By then, Hooker had pulled the main Union army back into a defensive position north of the Chancellorsville crossroads and Lee took a calculated risk to divert more of his formations to Fredericksburg. In the late afternoon, when the gathering Confederates outnumbered the isolated Federal Sixth Corps, Lee launched a series of attacks to destroy it. Close fighting extended into the night. The Federals fought well, but without any sign of support, they prudently retreated back across the Rappahannock River.

Just over 60 years would pass between the end of the Civil War and the time that a battlefield park would be established in Fredericksburg and Spotsylvania County. During that period, the hasty battlefield graves and burial trenches would be dug again and the dead removed to cemeteries.

> Before the streets were paved in the neighborhoods in front of Sunken Road and Marye's Heights, a hard rain would invariably wash Minie balls out of the soil. The Civil War is never very distant in Fredericksburg.

The community would resume life and attempt to rebuild. Fredericksburg residents discovered and removed skeletal remains, repaired homes blasted by artillery fire, and renewed industrial operations in buildings once used as hospitals. Reminders of the war were never far away though. People found ordnance in their gardens, in walls, or under floorboards. Intact projectiles could still function and sometimes did, jarred by careless handling or cooked-off when a building caught fire. Those who farmed the land routinely uncovered rusting equipment as they worked their fields and dumped the unwelcome detritus in fence corners. Construction workers in Fredericksburg got used to finding Union artillery projectiles that had been fired into town from battery positions in Stafford County. Before the streets were paved in the neighborhoods in front of Sunken Road and Marye's Heights, a hard rain would invariably wash Minie balls out of the soil. The Civil War is never very distant in Fredericksburg.[8]

The blackened land turned green again and the battlefields drew visitors. During the war and immediately afterward, there had been those who searched the scarred landscape for the remains of a husband, a father, or a son. Some were successful; many were not. The National Cemetery in Fredericksburg contains thousands of unknown soldiers and that had to be good enough for their families. Others, untouched by the war, also visited, drawn to places once obscure, but now become legendary.

In time, Civil War veterans began to revisit the places where they had struggled and survived. For an individual, war is a violent ordeal in the company of others who will forever be comrades. Their experiences became more understandable in the context of their regiments, brigades, and divisions, which constituted corps and then an army. The old soldiers were usually drawn to Gettysburg, if they had fought there, where victory had been clear and a private organization had been purchasing extensive portions of the battlefield. By the time national battlefield parks were established, veterans had already placed more than 300 monuments to their respective units on the Pennsylvania fields preserved to commemorate that great battle. Twenty five years after Appomattox, in 1890, President Benjamin Harrison, himself a Union veteran, signed a bill establishing Chickamauga/Chattanooga as a National Military Park, the nation's first. Over the next ten years, the Federal government brought three more military parks into being, at Shiloh, Gettysburg, and Vicksburg. Antietam also received Federal designation, but as an entity called a site. That convenient definition limited public acquisition of land to token tracts, where monuments could be erected. It appeared unnecessary to purchase the rest of the battlefield landscape, which was being actively farmed and would likely remain that way. This supposedly cost-effective idea would also be followed at Fredericksburg, but the concept turned out to be an illusion. Future generations would have to expend substantial time and treasure to finish the task of preserving battlefields initially established under what came to be called the Antietam Plan.[9]

In the early twentieth century, the battlefields around Fredericksburg remained as they had been before the war, integral parts of a rural region characterized by farms and woodlands and a river town where the local population found employment in mills and factories. Time had softened abandoned trenches and many miles of earthworks had been filled in by farmers reclaiming their croplands. Other farms remained neglected, their owners having moved on, their fields become overgrown. Immediately after the war, a National Cemetery had been established in Fredericksburg for the Union dead. A local organization called the Ladies Memorial Association had seen to the burial of the Confederate dead. Some of the places where prominent soldiers had been killed also called out for remembrance. One of the first local battlefield monuments had been a large granite boulder moved to the site on the Orange Turnpike (modern State Route 3) where Stonewall Jackson had been wounded. In 1888, Confederate veterans erected a more finished monument to Jackson, the impetus for its construction a similar edifice placed by Union veterans the year before, marking the site at Spotsylvania Court House where Union General John Sedgwick had been killed.[10]

In the post-war years, growing numbers of visitors found their way to the National Cemetery and to the Fredericksburg area battlefields. Such visits began to fall off though, when actual Military Parks were established elsewhere. In places receiving federal attention, well-researched markers and tablets gave visitors detailed information on what had occurred on the ground where they stood. The battlefields became attractive places to visit. Local boosters seeking viable economic opportunities in the struggling region noted that no battlefield park existed in Virginia, even though a substantial part of the war had been fought there. In 1896, the Fredericksburg city council urged its Congressional delegation to help establish a national battlefield park, "such as has been established at Gettysburg and other places." In 1898, the General Assembly of the Commonwealth of Virginia incorporated "the Fredericksburg and adjacent national battlefields memorial park association of Virginia," to acquire, mark, and preserve Fredericksburg area battlegrounds. The Spanish American War and then World War One, however, interrupted the momentum for a new park. In addition, Fredericksburg was just one of many other places with battlefields that were lobbying Congress for a new national park. Finally, in 1924, Congress created a Battlefield Park Commission to study the battlegrounds at Fredericksburg and acted on its recommendation, in 1927, to finally direct the War Department to establish a military park that included the area's several battlefields.[11]

While the Federal government had been considering how to proceed at Fredericksburg, the Fredericksburg and Spotsylvania chapters of the United Daughters of the Confederacy (UDC) had organized and coordinated their resources to set five markers in the Fredericksburg area, similar in style to 59 markers that a private group had placed in and around Richmond. The UDC markers were located at Fredericksburg, Chancellorsville, the Wilderness, and Spotsylvania Court House. They erected the fifth marker at Salem Church. Some few memorials had been placed by those who had fought the war, but by 1927, when a national battlefield park came into existence at Fredericksburg, the living memory of the Civil War had passed. Commemorative markers were being placed by later generations who knew of the war through the lens of history.[12]

The UDC markers reflect the memory of the war as it was popularly understood at the time. The Fredericksburg tablet, for example, makes sure to state that "Lee defeated the Federals," while generously admitting that the Union attacks had been "gallant." The Chancellorsville tablet, stolen in the 1970s and still missing, noted that "Lee defeated the Army of the Potomac," while also recalling Stonewall Jackson as "Lee's greatest lieuten-

In 1927, the United Daughters of the Confederacy placed this bronze panel at Salem Church. The narrative is sentimental in the extreme, but the dates of May 3 and 4, 1863 are accurate in describing the extent of the fighting in that area.

ant." The Wilderness panel repeats a wishful "Lee defeated" Lieutenant General Ulysses S. Grant, but the reality of 1864 could not carry that theme much further. The panel at Spotsylvania Court House displays phrases like "unyielding heroism" and "devotion to duty and principle," rather than acknowledging a dying Confederacy.[13]

Within this celebration of Southern victories, the Chancellorsville campaign received recognition on two out of five panels. The now missing marker at the Chancellorsville crossroads memorialized that portion of the campaign that occurred on May 2 and 3, giving no indication that the battle actually began on May 1, a few miles to the east. The Salem Church panel refers to the fighting on May 3 and 4, which acknowledges the heavy fighting around Fredericksburg, which is the area's fifth battlefield. Though the dates are accurate, the text strays into a theme of reconciliation, quite popular at the time, favorably comparing the patriotism of "the followers of Lee" with that of "the followers of Grant." Ulysses S. Grant, of course, was nowhere near Fredericksburg until 1864 and never came within cannon range of Salem

Church. The UDC panel is in the right place, with the right dates, but the rest does not impart any useful information about actual events.[14]

The good ladies of the UDC were not the only ones reflecting the popular interpretations of the day. When the Federal government finally established the Fredericksburg and Spotsylvania County Battlefields Memorial Military Park, the War Department's battlefield custodians did not challenge the historic themes that had become prevalent in the South. As an example, the name of Confederate General James Longstreet is noticeably absent on the markers placed along the Fredericksburg battlefield trench lines. In December 1862, Longstreet was one of two corps commanders in Robert E. Lee's Army of Northern Virginia. The other was Stonewall Jackson. In the post-war years, Longstreet had had the temerity to suggest that Lee might have made errors at Gettysburg. The Southern commander's outraged defenders responded by vilifying Longstreet as the culprit who not only caused that battle in Pennsylvania to be lost, but had thereby doomed the Confederacy. In a war fought with ink, the viewpoint of an infallible Lee and a legendary Jackson prevailed in popular and even scholarly history. The War Department marked the trenches in the sector held by Jackson's corps as "Jackson's Line." The trenches held by Longstreet's corps are marked with the names of his division commanders. The name Longstreet was thus neatly excised from the narrative by the federal agency that had once sought to use battlefields parks as places for professional development.[15]

At its first managed battlefields, the War Department had systematically interpreted the ground to create settings for military study. The government had a wealth of data in its *Official Records of the Union and Confederate Armies* and was also able to correspond with the veterans who had written the after-action reports that constitute so much of those records. This exchange helped to address conflicts within the documentation and confirm details of battle in relation to the terrain. Very specific markers, accurately placed, dot the landscapes at Gettysburg, Shiloh, Chickamauga/Chattanooga, and Vicksburg. They are not without the occasional error, but they remain extremely useful to those who study those battlefields today. At the Fredericksburg and Spotsylvania County Battlefields Memorial Military Park, as it was first called, the War Department still had a wealth of archival data and conducted considerable research that guided the initial land acquisition, but the stock market crash of 1929 interrupted everything. The expenditure of resources that provided the interpretation of the earlier battlefield parks was not going to be repeated at Fredericksburg. Instead of the thorough analysis of the Fredericksburg area battlegrounds as fields of professional study, the War Department only had the means to identify trench lines and the occasional terrain feature. Of the two battles fought on the same ground at Fredericksburg, the War Department markers also identified only the 1862 battlefield. In 1933, when the recently formed National Park Service assumed custody of the Park, the interpretation of the battle of Chancellorsville emphasized what had occurred in the wooded country a dozen miles west of Fredericksburg.[16]

Of the 2,100 acres the War Department included in the new National Park, only 110 acres had been acquired at Fredericksburg. The protected terrain there was limited to the Confederate position in the Sunken Road/Marye's Heights area, including the National Cemetery, and the Confederate trenches that extend from Telegraph Hill (Lee's Hill), through Howison Hill, and on to Prospect Hill. This available land proved too limiting for clearly presenting the battleground to the public and these conditions had not changed when the National Park Service assumed responsibility for the military park. Further, as the nation tried to overcome the Great Depression, New Deal work programs emphasized getting people back to work. An influx of Federal resources, though quite welcome, was directed to upgrading the Park's infrastructure, its roads and facilities, rather than expanding the federal holdings.[17]

During that period of well-funded construction projects, the National Park Service was still able to engage in basic research. A group of historians developed numerous battle maps, including a series for the second battle of Fredericksburg. The acquisition of land at Fredericksburg, however, remained limited, its cost having been much more than acreage could be had in remote corners of Spotsylvania County. The National Park Service would develop a handsome set of cast aluminum interpretive panels, which had identifying medallions for each of the four battlefields, but a fifth medallion would never be developed to identify and interpret the second Fredericksburg battle. On its relatively small holdings around Sunken Road/Marye's Heights, there would be only a few instances when the second battle would get mentioned–a wayside panel at Lee's Hill and a marker at a Confederate battery position in the National Cemetery.[18]

The emphasis on December 1862 at Fredericksburg appears to have carried over into a later national inventory of Civil War battlefields. In the

1990s, the Civil War Sites Advisory Commission engaged in a comprehensive effort to identify battlefields and evaluate the potential for their preservation. The Commission's report included the 3 May 1863 battlefields of Second Fredericksburg and Salem Church, but reference to the May 4 battle that occurred just west of Fredericksburg is a garbled mess in the Salem Church entry of the Commission's final report. When queried by the author, the American Battlefield Protection Program staff insisted that the 4 May 1863 battle had only been a retreat skirmish. For all its sentimentality, the UDC marker at Salem Church, erected in 1927, is more accurate about the scope of the Chancellorsville campaign than the national inventory that is used as a database to identify historic terrain when roads and other development is planned.[19]

> While significant portions of the Chancellorsville battleground west of Salem Church have been memorialized and preserved, the unprotected battlefields east of Salem Church have become houses, businesses, churches, and schools.

The events that unfolded in and around Fredericksburg in April and May of 1863 had not always been so fully forgotten. In 1910, an army officer named John Bigelow, Jr. studied Hooker's preparations and subsequent campaign through the official War Department records. His book, *The Campaign of Chancellorsville*, is recognized as a classic use of the correspondence and after-action reports that are still the cornerstone of Civil War research. Bigelow was systematic and thorough and included Second Fredericksburg, Salem Church, and the May 4 battles in his narrative. The wealth of Civil War source material has always supported such detailed study, but where the terrain is overgrown or difficult to access, the historic studies become vague. There have also been those less conscientious than Bigelow, whose omissions were masked by a compelling writing style.[20]

When the Federal government established its new military park in Fredericksburg and in Spotsylvania County, Douglas Southall Freeman was in the process of publishing what would become a very popular biography of Robert E. Lee. In volumes two and three (of four), he emphasized the battle fought on May 2 and 3, 1863 as Lee's greatest. He spent little time on Salem Church and even less on the battle fought on May 4. Freeman intimated that Lee's handling of the Chancellorsville campaign had been "flawless," which he would not have been able to claim if he had delved into the events that followed Lee's triumphal ride into the Chancellorsville clearing. Rather than being challenged for his selective use of source material, Freeman received the 1935 Pulitzer Prize.[21]

Freeman also received praise for the concept of maintaining the fog of war for his readers, providing only the information that Lee had as the story unfolds. Many other writers have embraced this idea and it has become a staple of Southern historiography. Divorcing military history from its underlying political context conveniently allows a writer to tell a very immediate and exciting story, while avoiding having to discuss any embarrassing background details, such as the political reality that the Confederate states were rebelling against the United States government in order to perpetuate a slave society. Tactical studies need not conform to some inappropriate political correctness, but military history has always had a practical aspect to it and to avoid unpleasant details is a disservice to the form.

Most visitors to the Fredericksburg battlefield do not realize there was a second battle fought in May 1863 on the same ground as the battle fought in December 1862. Further, they do not typically know that most of the earthworks they see were not there in December. Artillery positions had been dug, but the infantry trenches were established after the winter battle and actually fought over during the Chancellorsville campaign. For a visitor following the tour route, there is no indication that the Federal army attacked and broke through the Confederate works at Lee's Hill and Howison Hill, on May 3, 1863. While significant portions of the Chancellorsville battleground west of Salem Church have been memorialized and preserved, the unprotected battlefields east of Salem Church have become houses, businesses, churches, and schools. The historic community of Fredericksburg has done what communities do–it has grown, to accommodate the needs of succeeding generations on what was once a bloody landscape.[22]

The historic Salem Church illustrates how battlefield terrain left unprotected is easily lost. Built in 1844, the bullet-marked brick sanctuary has been preserved on a very small bit of ground and a visitor today finds little indication of the scope of the fighting there. Preservation advocates like to use Salem Church as an example of a battlefield being consumed by pavement and houses, but little effort has actually gone into trying to acquire and preserve that ground. When finite resources were available to buy bat-

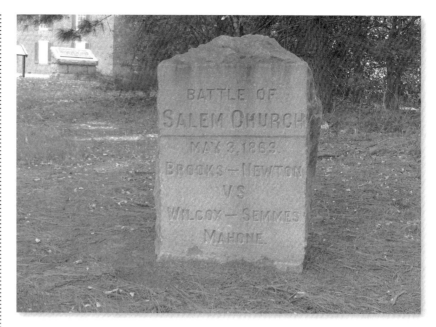

The Reverend James Power Smith placed this small stone marker at Salem Church in 1903. It notes the brigade commanders who fought at Salem Church.

tlefield terrain, they could be used to acquire and protect more land elsewhere, and were.[23]

The potential loss of the Salem Church battlefield was not always clear, but it did become inevitable. In 1903, the Reverend James Power Smith, a former aide-de-camp to Stonewall Jackson had placed a series of dressed stones around the Fredericksburg battlefields, marking sites related to Lee and Jackson. He placed one of them near Salem Church that identified the brigade commanders, three Confederate and two Union, who fought there. There are also two other stone monuments nearby, one erected by veterans of the 23rd New Jersey Regiment and the other by men of the 15th New Jersey, placed in 1907 and 1909 respectively. In 1927, the United Daughters of the Confederacy also dedicated a commemorative metal tablet there. At the time, the surrounding land remained rural and these various markers were token guides for visitors who could see and examine the battlefield around them. Within a few decades though, new interstate highways exerted a dynamic influence that severely compromised the battlefield context.[24]

In 1946, a steel and concrete bridge over the Rappahannock River carried the U.S. Route 1 Bypass (Jefferson Davis Highway) past Fredericksburg. Less than twenty years later, another bridge carried Interstate-95 over the Rappahannock. A development boom followed each new roadway. In the 1970s, children emerging from services at a newly built and larger Salem Church could still wander into the surrounding cow pastures and easily find small white objects exposed in the dirt–oxidized lead bullets from the violent days of May 3 and 4, in 1863. By the 1980s, the battleground around Salem Church had begun to succumb to development. Today, it is a minor tour stop surrounded by houses and shopping centers. The old church and its various markers have become the historic attractions rather than the actual battlefield.[25]

The relentless development that followed the new highways has not been a surprise, but it was not until the early 1970s that a newly-arrived chief historian for the Park began a concerted drive to acquire critical battlefield land threatened with imminent development. The Park staff had always been dedicated to protecting the land in its custody, but in 1969, four battlefields were interpreted on a mere 2,587 acres. The scattered Federal acreage had been relatively cohesive in a rural setting, but new houses and commercial strips were intruding into the historic ground that visitors came to experience. The Antietam method that called for the acquisition of limited tracts of historic ground had proved entirely inadequate and left virtually everything else vulnerable to loss.[26]

The Park historians began to painstakingly build up the Federal holdings and by 1979 there were more than 6,000 acres under Federal protection. The staff spent those years seeking donations of land, pursuing acquisition in fee simple, and even swapping land of lesser importance to obtain land more critical to the Park's needs. This necessity of having to choose some land over others has been the hard reality of working in Fredericksburg, where development pressure increases significantly each time the well-funded road builders put down a new highway.[27]

In the Fredericksburg area, land parcels are often selling only one more time before being built upon. In this context, limited resources dictated that many places would never receive the attention afforded better known terrain elsewhere. Salem Church, as noted previously, sits closer to Interstate-95 than the battlefields of May 1-3, 1863. Limited funds expended at Salem Church would have not been available to obtain considerably more acreage farther west, so the real efforts to preserve ground were judiciously pursued to the west. To build a park that could tell a story to visitors, it was necessary to engage in a type of preservation triage, acquiring important ground through whatever means necessary, risking the loss of other ground until funds became available, and accepting the inevitable loss of other places. When non-profit organizations formed in the 1990s to help in the effort to acquire and protect historic land around Fredericksburg, they too engaged in the same selection method, recognizing that they had only a limited period in which to acquire terrain before it disappeared under rooftops and pavement. Opportunity was not a sufficient reason to expend precious resources. The historic significance of one site over another had to be weighed for each decision to acquire and protect, and there was always the risk that an important site would be lost to development because scarce resources had already been expended in another less important location.[28]

Some decry Fredericksburg as insensitive to its history, allowing development to occur on important sites, but the Civil War had impacted everything. The community has had to pragmatically figure out how to live on intimate terms with its historic setting. The urban battlefield in downtown Fredericksburg is still a vibrant small town neighborhood, occupied today as it was in the 1860s by families and businesses. Residents replaced bullet riddled weatherboards and patched over holes punched by cannonballs, but chipped chimney bricks still show where small arms fire was intense. During the intervening century and a half, the houses have expanded and new buildings have been constructed, but veterans, if any were still alive to visit, would readily recognize the buildings of their time as well as the pattern of the alleys and streets through which they fought. Fredericksburg was also an industrial town when the armies came and many of those larger buildings remain, used as hospitals during the war, returned to industrial work afterward, and adapted to new uses today. The canals that powered those industries also survive, one of them a dry feature within a riverside park, and the other still carrying water, forcing the later road network to accommodate its course.[29]

Not all changes have been destructive to battlefield features either. New roads have redirected some development patterns and many areas of the historic landscape that were once busy places have been bypassed by the modern age. Though historic features in these newly remote places have devolved back to nature, their presence helps us to read the land. River crossings, for instance, can be pinpointed with great accuracy because they were mapped by military men in relation to man-made features such as mills and canals, whose stone foundations have not moved. Remnants of trenches and gun pits survive, as do traces of ante-bellum roads and routes cut by Federal engineers. In wooded areas, thick vegetation covers these wartime features, but they become visible in the winter months when the leaves are down. Earthworks and the expedient wartime roads began to erode almost immediately upon construction, but remnants of those cuts in the earth can still be found. Where they have grown faint, a light snow on the ground often provides a useful contrast when looking for them today.

With study, the physical evidence of the May 1863 battlefields becomes substantial. A few timbers from a mill dam on Hazel Run, kept from microbial degradation by being immersed in water, shows us exactly where several regiments of Georgians splashed through a mill pond, on the morning of May 4. A line of cedar trees in an industrial park marks the old road to Braehead, an ante-bellum mansion where Federals attacked on the morning of May 3. A slight drop in the land through a residential neighborhood is the area where Captain Oliver Wendell Holmes took shelter with his regiment that day and where he sustained his third wound of the war. An alley behind a row of houses in another neighborhood runs along the top of an embankment that sheltered a brigade of infantry as it waited to attack the seemingly impregnable Sunken Road. Within the National Park boundary, a draw that runs up and into the National Cemetery was used by Vermont troops to ascend the back slope of Marye's Heights and capture a section of Confederate guns. This approach is separate from another draw on the other side of the hill (also within the National Park) where Maine troops crashed over the stone wall, bayoneted Confederate defenders, and then surged up on to the heights.

The battlefield terrain within the modern development is still evident, but it also challenges our perceptions about how battlefields should look. The Civil War was fought across a nineteenth century landscape and we expect the battlefields we visit to be verdant. Anything less is characterized as lost, desecrated for those who insist on the burden of reverence. Regardless of its condition though, its story may still be relevant, perhaps even critical to an understanding of an overall battle or campaign. Military history is a challenge to research and present because of the inherent confusion of combat. For military historians, the terrain itself becomes an important resource, re-

State Route 3 and its related development is intrusive on the Salem Church battlefield, but the gentle slope that Federal troops encountered has not changed and the cut through the hilltop also remains clearly evident.

vealing insights that are not apparent in an archive. An historian must examine the terrain he or she seeks to write about, regardless of its condition.

Finding the battleground in the middle area between Fredericksburg and Salem Church for instance, is an exercise in trying to discern the importance of much-altered land. That terrain, fought over on May 3 and May 4, has changed considerably as a result of the development that followed creation of a highway interchange at Interstate-95 and State Route 3. The obscured historic context is extensive, stretching north across the Rappahannock River, into the area where the winter campaign known as the Mud March occurred in January 1863. At that time, the Federal commander had been Major General Ambrose E. Burnside, who had led his army to disaster at Fredericksburg the month before. The Mud March has become a symbol of abject failure and led to Burnside's removal from command, but his plan reflected careful preparation, which is evident when we look at his objective, the high ground west of Fredericksburg.[30]

Burnside had directed his forces toward a crossing of the Rappahannock River near Banks Ford, which is the first break in the river bluffs above Fredericksburg. The plan was to then occupy the plateau west of Fredericksburg that is now under the pavement and buildings of the Route 3 commercial corridor. Before launching his army into the January weather, Burnside had worked with Brigadier General Marsena Patrick to determine a viable campaign objective. Patrick had been in Fredericksburg in the spring of 1862, during the Peninsula campaign, and he and Burnside came to realize that if they could occupy the elevated ground west of Fredericksburg, the Federals would be well-positioned to receive a Confederate attack. Weather foiled Burnside's advance and the effort ended in failure, but Federal forces would be back in the spring, occupying the ground west of Fredericksburg on May 3 and 4. The Federals established a formidable defensive position there, as Burnside had anticipated being able to do in January.[31]

This favorable terrain is cut by the interstate highway and covered by shopping centers and subdivisions, but the overall plateau is evident and battlefield features sometimes reveal themselves here as well. Each day, thousands of drivers on William Street pass by a prominent embankment where the road cuts through the hilltop. That cut was remarked upon by both Union and Confederate soldiers who fought through there on May 4, 1863. In a nearby subdivision, two Confederate guns pits occupy the front yard of a comfortable home. Confederates held that position in December 1862, Federals held it in May 1863. A sunken road that once sheltered Union infantry in another subdivision is no longer a road, but rather a depression across several back yards. An ante-bellum mansion called Idlewild still stands near a subdivision of the same name, held by a Federal skirmish line on May 4 and occupied by Robert E. Lee as his headquarters that evening.

For individual soldiers, war is a continuum of violence moving toward an unknowable end. The men operating in Fredericksburg during the 1863 Chancellorsville campaign moved across fields where the bodies of comrades poked out of the dirt, the result of hasty burials in December 1862. As noted above, some of that contested terrain is preserved within the Fredericksburg and Spotsylvania National Military Park, but visitors are oriented to the 1862 ground with little references to the 1863 action. Historic interpretations established in the 1930s and the practical aspects of trying to acquire land within a volatile real estate market appear to have limited the attention given to terrain associated with the second battle of Fredericksburg.

In practice, history is a discussion, an ongoing effort informed by research and discovery of new evidence. The battlefields themselves have the potential to reveal insights and are integral to this discussion. Land can be altered though, getting clear cut and developed, or neglected and overgrown. It gets subdivided and built upon, the earth moved around to enhance drainage and flattened to facilitate construction. The National Park Service has carefully restored the wartime configuration and vegetative cover of the battlefield lands in its custody, which has considerably enhanced their interpretation. Non-profit organizations engaged in battlefield preservation have done the same for lands they have acquired. The battlefield terrain beyond the preservation boundary, however, has very often changed and requires some level of forensic geography before we can begin to understand its significance.

In 1996, the Central Virginia Battlefields Trust formed to help acquire and preserve ground related to the battles at Fredericksburg, Chancellorsville, the Wilderness, and Spotsylvania Court House. Its first purchase was a significant portion of Marye's Heights, including the draw where elements of the Sixth Corps gained the hilltop on May 3, 1863. In 2001, the organization acquired a representative part of the May 4, 1863 battlefield along Smith Run, in Fredericksburg. The CVBT also helped to purchase the terrain known as the Slaughter Pen Farm. All of these places, and others, were fought over during the second battle of Fredericksburg. There are limited opportunities to acquire more land related to the second Fredericksburg battle, but there are still places where the interpretation of preserved as well as unprotected land can be expanded to better understand this fifth major battle in the Fredericksburg area.

Over the course of the Chancellorsville campaign, the Union Sixth Corps sustained 26 percent of the overall losses suffered by the Army of the Potomac between April 29 and May 5, 1863. The Federal troops operating in and around Fredericksburg also captured three Confederate battle flags and ten artillery pieces. They lost none of their own, although two of the guns were later recaptured. The Confederates confronting the Union Sixth Corps also suffered casualties that constituted 26-29 percent of Southern losses for the overall campaign. The operations east of Salem Church were not a mere sideshow and additional study can expand our understanding of the Chancellorsville campaign beyond the Lee-Jackson-Hooker narrative.[32]

The Fredericksburg and Spotsylvania National Military Park once had a distinctive set of wayside panels that provided visitors a self-guided tour through its several battlefields. They were cast aluminum panels, with raised letters and graphics, erected between two wooden posts, and included excellent maps that were oriented to the view visible to the reader. Initiated in the 1930s, the same design was used by the Park staff in subsequent decades when new lands were added to the federal holdings or new vistas established. Of interest are the battlefield identifiers, graphic medallions that made clear which battlefield was being discussed, which proved useful in those places where historic terrain overlapped, such as Wilderness and Chancellorsville. Three battlefield brands are shown here. The fourth identifies the Spotsylvania Court House battlefield, where there is no overlap with other battlegrounds. In recent years, the metal panels have begun to be replaced by colorful graphics embedded in fiberglass panels. The concept of individual battlefield brands, however, could be revived if the second Fredericksburg battlefield were to be interpreted where the first Fredericksburg battle has been emphasized since the National Military Park was established.

∾ NOTES ∾

1. *The War of the Rebellion: A Compilation of the Official Records of the Union and Confederate Armies*, 128 vols. (Washington D.C., 1880-1901), Series 1, Vol. 25, 599 (hereafter cited as *OR*.. All references in Series 1, Volume 25).
2. *Hard Marching Every Day: The Civil War Letters of Private Wilbur Fisk, 1861-1865*, eds. Emil and Ruth Rosenblatt (University Press of Kansas, 1992), 78; *OR*, 599.
3. *OR*, 609, 611.
4. *Hard Marching*, 79.
5. *OR*, 842, 847.
6. *Hard Marching*, 79
7. *OR*, 603, 842.
8. "Civil War Shot Makes Big Noise," *Winchester (VA) Evening Star*, 19 January 1915; "Woolen Factory Costing $128,000 Destroyed by Fire," *Virginia Herald*, 25 October 1875; Amy Satterthwaite, "Civil War Shot Found in Kenmore," *Free Lance-Star* (Fredericksburg, VA), 22 February 1989; "Burst Up at Hunter & Frost's Foundry," *Virginia Herald*, 29 April 1872. There was more ordnance collected and disposed of than just the rounds referenced in these dramatic stories. This article indicates that the local foundry had a department that routinely disposed of unexploded ordnance brought in from around the region. Jean Rayman, interview by author, Fredericksburg, VA, 23 June 2015. Jean's family owned a small patch of land north of the Chancellorsville clearing. She remembers how they routinely found bayonets, bullets, grapeshot, cannonballs as well as unexploded ordnance. Her father was not sentimental about all of the old metal in the ground and was happy to let relic hunters search the property and haul away what they found. Her father also worked at Mary Washington College, in Fredericksburg, and encountered numerous Parrott shells, fired by Union artillery against the Confederate guns deployed on the ridge where the College was built. The author's neighbor, Mrs. Othello Hayden recounted how heavy rains would wash out Minie balls in the ditches along the edges of the properties before curbs and gutters were installed and the streets paved.
9. Department of the Interior, National Park Service, *Civil War Sites Advisory Commission, Report on the Nation's Battlefields, Technical*

Volume I: Appendices (Washington D.C., 1993, revised 1999), 160-161.

10. J.H Beadle, "At Spottsylvania," Knoxville (TN) *Daily Journal and Tribune*, 21 July 1895. Pfanz, *Through Eyes of Stone*, 122-123, 126-132, 207-210.
11. Fredericksburg City Council, resolution urging the City's Congressional delegation to support formation of a Fredericksburg battlefields park, 21 February 1896, (Fredericksburg, VA); Virginia Assembly. *Acts and Joint Resolutions Passed by the General Assembly of the State of Virginia, Session of 1897-98* (Richmond, VA), 364-366; Department of the Interior, National Park Service, *At the Crossroads of Preservation and Development: A History of Fredericksburg and Spotsylvania National Military Park*, by Joan M. Zenzen, (2011), 29-38.
12. The UDC markers are of the same design as a set of 59 markers placed in and around Richmond by the Battlefield Markers Association. They consist of a square stone base, with a cast metal plaque on top, set at an angle for ease of reading.
13. National Park Service, Fredericksburg and Spotsylvania National Military Park, *History Through Eyes of Stone: A Survey of Civil War Monuments Near Fredericksburg, Virginia*, by Donald C. Pfanz (Fredericksburg, VA 1983, revised 2006), 25-29.
14. Ibid.
15. A park road called Lee Drive takes visitors past several miles of Confederate trenches. The cast iron signs placed by the War Department in the early 1920s are still in place. Five of them identify where Stonewall Jackson's troops held the line and read: "Confederate Trenches–Jackson's Line." Along the trenches held by James Longstreet's troops, there are four signs that read "Confederate Trenches–McLaws' Division," two signs that read "Confederate Trenches–Pickett's Division," and one sign that reads "Confederate Line–Hood's Division."
16. Zenzen, *At the Crossroads*, 97-98.
17. Zenzen, *At the Crossroads*, 32, 36.
18. Library of Congress, Report of the Librarian of Congress, for the Fiscal Year Ending June 30, 1934 (Washington D.C., Government Printing Office, 1934), 105-106. The National Park Service's chief historian was Verne E. Chatelain and the staff working in the Division of Maps consisted of Colonel Thomas L. Heffernan, Major Joseph Mills Hanson, Mr. Edward Steere, and Miss Ruth Graham. This group developed a set

of detailed maps that track the Sixth Corps' movements from 29 April–3 May 1863. Zenzen, *At the Crossroads*, 59-60.
19. Department of the Interior, National Park Service, *Civil War Sites Advisory Commission, Report on the Nation's Battlefields, Technical Volume II: Battle Summaries* (Washington D.C., 1993, revised 1998), 171.
20. John Bigelow, Jr., *The Campaign of Chancellorsville: A Strategic and Tactical Study* (New Haven: Yale University Press, 1910).
21. Zenzen, *At the Crossroads*, 98. Douglas Southall Freeman, *R.E. Lee*, vol. 3 (New York: Charles Scribner's Sons, 1935), 2. Dr. Freeman was artfully passive in asserting that Chancellorsville had been a "flawless" victory. He stated that Lee himself would never have dreamed of describing his victory in such terms, but that military critics had done so, thus neatly absolving both Lee and himself from any responsibility for that conclusion.
22. Zenzen, *At the Crossroads*, 163, 182-183.
23. Department of Commerce, *Old Salem Church Historic Structure Report*, by Ralph Happel (Washington D.C., 1968), 12. Zenzen, *At the Crossroads*, 377-378.
24. Pfanz, *Through Eyes of Stone*, 11, 25-29, 38-39, 146-149.
25. James M. Pates, interview by author, Fredericksburg, VA, 24 June 2015. As a child, Jim attended services in the new Salem Church and remembers finding Minie balls in the cultivated land surrounding to the 1844 church.
26. Zenzen, *At the Crossroads*, 36.
27. Robert K. Krick, Chief Historian at FSNMP, was instrumental in focusing the Park's attention to acquiring more land while opportunities lasted, as noted in Zenzen, *At the Crossroads*, 276.
28. The author was a founding member of the Central Virginia Battlefields Trust in 1996 and served on its Board of Directors for 15 years. Like the National Park Service, the CVBT had to acknowledge that time and resources were limited when developing priorities for which parcels of land would be targeted for acquisition. When battlefield property outside the priority list became available, the Board had to weigh how quickly a deal could be concluded and a note paid off, so as not to jeopardize the acquisition of other, more critical lands. The Fredericksburg and Spotsylvania National Military Park has since grown to encompass more than 8,000 acres, but still interpreting only four battlefields rather than five.

29. Franklin Powell, interview by author, Fredericksburg, VA, 2 February 1997. Mr. Powell is a Fredericksburg contractor who renovated numerous buildings in downtown Fredericksburg. While working on a house at the corner of Caroline and Hawke Streets, where extensive street fighting had occurred on 11 December 1862, he found interior walls riddled with bullet holes that had been neatly wallpapered over. The owners had made the outer walls and the roof of the house weathertight, but replacing the interior walls would have been extravagant during the hard post-war years in Fredericksburg. The wallpaper worked very well to hide the evidence of violence.
30. David S. Sparks, ed., *Inside Lincoln's Army: The Diary of Marsena Rudolph Patrick, Provost Marshal General, Army of the Potomac* (New York: Thomas Yoseloff, 1964), 202-203.
31. A. Wilson Greene, *Morale, Maneuver, and Mud: The Army of the Potomac, December 16, 1862 – January 26, 1863*, in *The Fredericksburg Campaign: Decision on the Rappahannock*, ed. Gary W. Gallagher (Chapel Hill: University of North Carolina Press, 1995), 194-197. Francis Augustin O'Reilly, *The Fredericksburg Campaign: Winter War on the Rappahannock* (Baton Rouge: Louisiana State University Press, 2003), 473-474.
32. Stephen W. Sears, *Chancellorsville* (New York: Houghton Mifflin Company, 1996), 475-501. Sears has done an extensive analysis of casualties sustained during the Chancellorsville campaign. The Federal casualties on the battlefields east of Salem Church are mostly confined to the Union Sixth Corps. There were also some few hundred casualties sustained by the Union First Corps at the river crossing south of Fredericksburg between 29 April 29 and 1 May, before Hooker called them to Chancellorsville early on 2 May. Confederate casualties from the units detached to confront the Union Sixth Corps are readily calculated, but several other formations fought around Chancellorsville and then marched to Salem Church and Fredericksburg and reported their losses for the overall campaign rather than day by day. A reasonable estimate of Confederate losses east of Salem Church is between 3,500-4,000 men, which is 26-29 percent of the overall Confederate losses for the entire campaign.

On May 21, 1864, at Massaponax Church in Spotsylvania County, photographer Timothy O'Sullivan recorded three of the most famous images of the Civil War. These photographs focus on Generals Ulysses S. Grant and George G. Meade during a rest along the march from the battlefield of Spotsylvania Court House to the North Anna River. The third photo, above, presents the clearest image of the famous generals and prominent members of their staffs.

Identified in this photo are: 1) Lieutenant General Ulysses S. Grant, Commanding General United States Army; 2) Assistant Secretary of War Charles A. Dana; 3) Brigadier General John A. Rawlins, Chief of Staff of General Headquarters United States Army; 4) Major General George G. Meade, Commanding General Army of the Potomac; 5) Lieutenant Colonel Cyrus B. Comstock, aide-de-camp to General Grant; 6) Lieutenant Colonel Adam Badeau, Military Secretary to General Grant.

Southern Exposure
Medal of Honor Recipient Caught Straggling on the March

BY ERIC J. MINK

On May 21, 1864, in the midst of General Ulysses S. Grant's Overland Campaign, photographer Timothy O'Sullivan pulled an impressive and enviable media coup. From the balcony of Massaponax Church in Spotsylvania County, O'Sullivan took some of the most famous images of the Civil War. This series of photographs focuses on Grant, General George G. Meade and their respective staffs during a rest along the march from the battlefield of Spotsylvania Court House to the North Anna River. Although the high ranking officers formed O'Sullivan's subject, another individual of note appears in the photo. He had yet, however, to reach the attention of army leaders, but would one day receive the nation's highest military award—the Medal of Honor.

O'Sullivan exposed at least three photographs of the army commanders and the officers who served at their headquarters. The pews of the church had been pulled out into the yard and the officers gathered around them. The arrangement on the pews changed as some officers came and went, perhaps delivering dispatches and generally going about their business. In the first two images, General Grant is visible conferring with General Meade as well as writing a dispatch. On the outer edges of the group, onlookers peered in on the assembly while wagons belonging to the 5th Corps pass by in the background. Meanwhile, O'Sullivan had climbed into the upper part of the church and poked his camera through the southeast window. One passerby took note of what he witnessed and later wrote:

Southern Exposure

In the top photo, General Grant (identified by the arrow) is seen leaning over a pew conferring with General Meade, while the bottom photo shows him seated and presumably drafting an order or dispatch. Visible in the background can be seen the blurred wagon train of the Fifth Army Corps, as it passes the church and continues south.

Under the shade of some noble trees in front of Massaponax church, I was permitted to look upon a number of our generals in council, consulting some maps of the region through which we were moving. A crowd of curious eyes gathered around to look upon the noted faces for a moment, while from the gallery windows of the church I observed a photographic instrument seizing the rare chance. I quietly studied the faces of those men, whom the generations will delight to honor, and having photographed them for private use, passed on, leaving the chiefs in council. —Anonymous, "Notes of a Visit to the Army of the Potomac," in *The Huntingdon [Penn.] Globe*, June 29, 1864.

It is O'Sullivan's third photo that presents the clearest image of the famous gathering. It is also in this third image that another man of note is present. He was neither a general, nor a member of the headquarters entourage. A mere teenage private lurking in the background, he undoubtedly elicited no notice. He was destined, however, to become a highly respected soldier.

The National Tribune, a weekly newspaper published in Washington, D.C., served as the primary organ for Union veterans after the war. It was a place where they could publish their memories of wartime experiences or debate each other on recollections of wartime events. In the August 12, 1897 edition of the *Tribune,* there appeared the following letter, written by Leander Herron of St. Paul, Nebraska:

At Bethesda Church, about June 1, 1864, Gen. Grant and staff had their photographs taken while sitting in front of the church. The camera was in the second-story window. At this time I was returning to my regiment, having been overcome by heat and placed in an ambulance. I was but 15 years old. The assemblage attracted my attention. The photograph was taken while I was looking at the crowd just back of the two trees, and to the rear of Gen. Grant. My picture shows me with my knapsack on, and partly a side view.

GENERAL GRANT AND STAFF AT BETHESDA CHURCH. (SEE MAP, PAGE 296.) GENERAL GRANT IS SITTING WITH HIS BACK TO THE SMALLER TREE. (FROM A WAR-TIME PHOTOGRAPH.)

Leander Herron, formerly a private in Company C, 83rd Pennsylvania Infantry, claimed to be visible in one of the three photographs. Obviously, some of Herron's information is incorrect. The photo is not Bethesda Church in Hanover County, but is Massaponax Church. It was not taken on June 1, 1864 but was taken May 21. While widely published now, these images were not nearly as famous in the late nineteenth century. A woodcut of the third photo that appeared as an illustration in a *Century Magazine* article is likely what Herron saw. Published in 1887, the caption for the woodcut contains the same erroneous information.

As a member of the 83rd Pennsylvania Infantry, Herron fought with the 5th Army Corps, which is the organization passing Massaponax Church at the time O'Sullivan exposed the plates. There is nothing exceptional about Herron's wartime service, outside of his survival. He enlisted on December 10, 1863 in New Brighton, Pennsylvania, served through the final year and half of the war and mustered out on June 28, 1865. Herron's fame as a soldier came after the Civil War.

Not content with civilian life in Pennsylvania, Herron re-enlisted and headed west to the frontier. He held the rank of corporal in Company A, 3rd United States Infantry. On the evening of September 1, 1868, Herron left Fort Larned, Kansas to deliver mail and dispatches to Fort Dodge, a distance of about 75 miles. On his way, he passed a fatigue detail of four soldiers gathering wood for the fort. The following day, when Herron made the return trip to Fort Larned, Corporal Patrick Boyle of the 7th United States Cavalry rode with him. About 12 miles out from Fort Dodge, they heard the sound of gunfire. The fatigue party Herron had encountered the night before was being attacked by Indians. With pistols drawn, Herron and Boyle rode directly through the attackers and reached the besieged wood detail. Herron took control of the detail and the six men fought from behind a wagon. The mules had been killed, which rendered the detail immobile and the soldiers faced an estimated force of 50 Indians.

Herron decided that someone needed to ride back to Fort Dodge for help. Since Boyle had the fastest mount, he drew the assignment. Reduced to a party of five, the soldiers held off repeated attacks throughout the night. Their ammunition grew low and the men sustained wounds. As dawn approached, only Herron remained unharmed. Finally, as the defenders prepared to receive what would likely be a final attack, Boyle and reinforcements from Fort Dodge arrived. The attackers fled and the fatigue party was rescued. For his courage and decisiveness, Herron received the Medal of Honor, although not until 1919. The citation reads:

The President of the United States of America, in the name of Congress, takes pleasure in presenting the Medal of Honor to Corporal Leander Herron, United States Army, for on 2 September 1868, while serving with Company A, 3d U.S. Infantry, in action at Fort Dodge, Kansas. While detailed as mail courier from the fort, Corporal Herron voluntarily went to the assistance of a party of four enlisted men, who were attacked by about 50 Indians at some distance from the fort and remained with them until the party was relieved.

Upon the expiration of his term of enlistment in 1870, Herron left the army and returned to Pennsylvania. Over the following years, he bounced between his home state and the west, trying his hand at farming and working in the oil fields. Herron and his family eventually settled in St. Paul, Nebraska where they finally made their home. On April 5, 1937, Herron passed away and is buried in St. Paul's Elmwood Cemetery.

O'Sullivan captured quite a few historical figures in his Massaponax series. His subjects were the men making history that day. Behind the gold and gilt gathered around the pews, a straggling teenager, destined to also make his mark in the army, went unnoticed in the background.

Eric J. Mink
Fredericksburg, Va.

Index

A

Adams, Andrew B. 47
Adams, J. William 45, 73
Adams, Robert W. 36, 42-44, 80
Aler, George 39, 48, 86
Alexander, John B. 42
Allen, William 73
Anderson, John L. 62
Armat, C. 47
Ashby, Charles 22n

B

Bachschmid, Paul 19, 21n, 28n, 29n, 30n
Barton, Thomas B. 59, 76, 77
Barton, William S. 71, 75
Beale (Mr.) 58
Bigelow, John, Jr. 116
Bowering, B.F. 45, 47
Bradley, James H. 46-49, 51, 52, 54-56, 58-64, 66-72, 74, 75, 77-80, 82, 84-88, 92-98
Bragdon, Charles 48
Braxton, Carter M. 42, 48, 66, 67, 70, 83
Braxton, E.M. 47-49, 51-56, 58, 61-67, 71-74, 77, 78, 80, 81, 83-89, 92, 93, 95-98
Brophy, John E. 62
Burke, William 59
Burnside, Ambrose E. 122, 123

C

Cahill, Martin 62, 63, 96
Caldwell, Richard 48
Carmichael, George F. 36, 39
Carter, Edwin 40, 49, 59
Chablin, L.F. 76

Cheek, William F. 73
Chew, George F. 46, 48, 49, 52, 53, 55
Chew, John James 45, 47, 49, 55
Chew, Robert S. 49, 54, 55, 75
Cole, E. Dorsey 67, 68
Cole, James L. 62, 63, 67, 68, 70
Colquitt, Alfred 22n
Conway, W.P. 41, 50
Cox, James A. 62
Cunningham, William H. 36, 37, 42, 43, 45-49, 51, 54-56, 58, 60-62, 64-68, 70, 71, 74, 75, 79, 80, 83-87, 92, 93, 96-98

D

Dachrodt, Jacob 19, 23n, 29n
Dawes, (Captain) 78
Deshazo, William H. 98
Dignum, Robert 45
Dillard, W.U. 52
Doggett, L.B. 50
Doles, George 22n, 28n

E

Edington, John M. 48, 49
Edrington, Charles W. 62, 68, 98
Edrington, James M. 62
Edrington, John 62
Eilenberger, David 16, 25n

F

Ficklen, James B. 58, 59, 98
Fitzhugh, St. George R. 98
Ford, James W. 66, 68-74, 77, 80-85, 88, 92, 93, 97
Fortune, Albert 67
Francis (Mr.) 52
Fraser, John C. 107
Freeman, Douglas Southall 116
Frueauff, John F. 19, 23n, 29n

G

Gill, Beverly T. 36, 37, 39, 40, 42-47
Gilmer, J.W. 85
Glanz, Charles 8 (photo), 11, 16, 18, 21n, 26n, 27n, 29n
Goolrick, Peter 37
Gouldman, William 62
Grant, Lewis A. 106
Grant, Ulysses S. 113
Gravatt, George 37, 39-41, 43, 45-48, 50
Green, D. 59

H

Habersham, Fred 107
Hammack, R.C. 64
Hayes, James 59, 80, 96
Harris, B.G. 62
Harrison, Benjamin 111
Hart, Robert C. 62
Hart, Robert W. 41, 48, 51, 60, 70, 73, 83
Hatch, Sophia 103n
Haynie, Edward T. 68, 81, 82, 85, 88, 89
Hedinger, Peter 62, 63
Heinichen, Edward L. 59
Hermes, Harry B. 42, 55, 60
Herndon, Brodie S. 72, 73
Holmes, Oliver Wendell 121
Hooker, Joseph 9, 16, 109
Howe, Albion P. 106, 107
Huffman, Landon J. 42, 46, 48, 50, 71, 75
Hurkamp, John G. 36, 37, 39-49, 51, 56, 58-62, 66, 67, 69-72, 75, 77-80, 82-88, 92, 93, 95, 96, 98

I

Iverson, Alfred 22n

Index

J
Jackson, Thomas J. "Stonewall" 9-11, 108, 111, 112, 118
Jennings, William 16, 25n
Johnson, Andrew 34, 100n
Johnson, C.M. 71
Johnson (Col.) 97
Johnson, James 76
Johnston, Gabriel 70
Jones, (Dr.) 39

K
Kelley, J.H. 88
Kelly, J.H. 73
Keyser, R. 72
Knight, John L. 43
Knox, R.F. 72, 73
Knox, Thomas F. 36, 37, 40-43, 45, 47-50, 55, 56, 58-67, 69, 71, 73-75, 78, 80-82, 84, 85, 87, 88, 92, 93, 95, 96
Krick, Robert K. 127n
Kueger, Lewis 52
Kunsman, Peter 15, 25n

L
Lange, William 45
Larkin, John B. 62, 63, 85, 96, 97
Lee, Robert E. 9, 108, 112, 116, 123
Lincoln, Abraham 33
Little, A.A. 77
Little, William A. 36, 37, 39, 41-43, 45-48, 51, 53-56, 58, 61, 66-68, 70, 72, 73, 75, 77, 80-86, 93, 97, 98
Longstreet, James 114
Lowley, Joseph E. 82, 86

M
Magrath, Lewis O. 45
Marshall, William J. 77
Marye, John L. 43, 44, 59, 100n
Marye, John L., Jr. 74, 77, 78
McGuire, James 36, 37, 40-49, 51, 55, 56, 58-62, 64, 65, 68, 70-75, 77-88, 92, 93, 95-98
McKenney, A.S. 96
Miller, F.T. 52, 100n
Mills, Fannie E. 60
Minor, R.D. 84
Moon, William J. 65, 66
Morrison (Mr.) 58
Myer, J.H. 82

N
Neff, Henry 16, 26n
Norton, William H. 60

O
O'Neal, Edward 22n, 28n

P
Perry, Julient 38
Patrick, Marsena 123
Phillips, A.K. 36
Phillips, Margaret 36
Pierpont, Francis H. 33

R
Reeder, Howard 11, 13 (photo), 14, 21n, 29n, 30n
Revere, W.H. 98
Rible (Ribley, Ribly), John 14, 24n
Rice, Owen 14, 23n, 27n
Ricker, John 11, 12 (photo), 21n, 29n, 30n
Richardson, Samuel P. 77, 78, 81, 82, 84, 87, 92, 93
Rimel (Reimel, Reinell), Jacob 15, 25n

Roberts, T.W. 98
Rodes, Robert 22n
Rose, (Dr.) 39
Rowe, Absalom P. 47-52, 54, 56, 58, 60, 62-65, 67-69, 71-75, 79-81, 84, 85, 87, 88, 92, 93, 95, 97, 98

S

Sale, Rebecca 70
Samuel, A.E. 59
Sandt, Aaron 28n
Schofield, John A. (also shown as J.M. and S.M.) 74-76, 94, 95, 101n
Scott, Charles S. 36-40, 42-47, 50, 87, 88
Scott, John F. 86
Scott, William S. 36, 44, 82, 89
Sears, Hector 93-96, 103n
Sedgwick, John 105, 109, 111
Sener, James B. 39, 40, 43, 70, 71, 73, 85
Sener, Joseph W. 36, 37, 39-43, 45-47, 50-52, 55, 58-62, 65, 67-75, 77-81, 83-86
Shepherd, Charles 62
Shepherd, George W. 36, 37, 42, 43, 46, 47
Slaughter, Montgomery 36, 37, 39, 40, 42-56, 59-69, 71-75, 77-83, 85-89, 92, 93, 95-98
Smith, James Power 118
Smith, William C. 62
Solan (Mr.) 54
Stephens, E.N. 70

T

Tackett, John E. 44, 47-52, 55, 56, 58, 63, 65, 66
Taylor, Clay 62
Taylor, James A. 48, 49, 96, 98
Timberlake, George H. 68, 72, 96, 97
Timberlake, John S.G 48, 96

V

von Gilsa, Leopold 23n 27n
von Steinwehr, Adolph 18, 28n

W

Walker, Alexander 36, 71, 101n
Wallace, C. Wistar 58, 82
Wallace, J. Gordon 36, 39, 48
Wallace, W.C. 82
Wallace, Stryker 11, 25n, 29n, 30n
Weaver, Ethan A. 24 (photo)
Weaver, William H. 24
Wellford, B.R. 56
Wellford, C.C. 56
Wheeler, Mary M. 63
White, Jesse 56, 59, 72
Wissner, H. 56
Wroten, George W. 47-49, 51, 52, 54, 56, 58-60, 62, 64, 65, 67-71, 73, 74, 78, 80, 86, 88, 90, 92, 93, 95-98

Y

Young, John James 37, 39-43, 45, 47-49, 51, 52, 54, 56, 58-63, 66-68, 71, 74, 79, 81, 82, 84, 85, 87, 88, 93, 96